Too Many
Mules Riding *in the*
Wagon

Prophetic Preaching for Church Ministry Engagement

by

Frederick M. Gillespie, D.Min.

ISBN-978-1-960853-80-6

Liberation's Publishing LLC
Columbus - Mississippi

Too Many
Mules *in the*
Wagon

**Prophetic Preaching for Church Ministry
Engagement**

"In all thy ways acknowledge him, And he shall direct thy paths." - Proverbs 3:6 (KJV)

"And we have seen and do testify that the Father sent the Son to be the Saviour of the world." - I John 4:14 (KJV)

Table of Contents

Acknowledgement

I am thankful for all members of the congregations I have served or currently serving, Zion Springs Baptist, New Hebron Baptist, Pilgrim Baptist, and New Bethel Baptist. You have supported me from the beginning of my spiritual journey and your continued support and encouragement has proven to be invaluable. Thanks to all those who served on the PPG and critiqued my sermons: Albert, Althea, Arlander, Ashley, Clarence, Danny, Don, Greg, John, Michael, Nekitta, Shelia, and Tito. I am indebted to you and owe you a tremendous debt of gratitude. I am a much better preacher because of your feedback, suggestions, and critiques. A very heartfelt thank you to Dr. James Robinson who read and provided invaluable feedback on this project. I am in awe of your spirit, attitude, and giftedness. You are a true inspiration.

Finally, a very special thank you to Alana. Your love, support, encouragement, and prayers have meant the world to me. You allowed me to take the time and space to read, write, and preach. Your presence made the journey more manageable and enjoyable than it would have been without you. I love you, Beautiful. Thank you to my mother, Warzella. Your encouragement and belief in me have been invaluable. After all these years I am still trying to make you proud and live up to the love you have shown me for fifty-seven years. I also hope and pray that this project will not be an embarrassment to you.

I dedicate this work to my deceased grandparents, Willie and Sallie Gillespie, and Eugene and Elnora Bailey. They instilled in me the importance and the power of a good education. None of them achieved the academic success I am attempting to achieve, however, the lessons they taught me are still present with me to this day. They taught and instilled within me the importance of accepting Jesus Christ as my Lord and Savior. They exemplified and presented a discipleship model for me to aspire to. I am where I am because of the seed they planted when I was just a child.

Chapter One

My Grandfather's Mules

My grandfather, Eugene Bailey, Sr., had seventeen children—ten boys and seven girls. He supported his family first as a sharecropper in rural northern Mississippi and then as a farmer. As a sharecropper and farmer, he never owned a tractor; he owned mules. My mother can name seventeen mules that he owned from her childhood. I only remember the last two mules he owned. One of my best childhood memories is riding in the wagon, driven by my grandfather, and being pulled by the two mules. When my grandfather plowed the fields with his mules, the mules were pulling the plow. When my grandfather needed to use the wagon, the mules were pulling the wagon from the front. According to my mother and me, my grandfather never allowed any of his mules to ride in a wagon. They were always in front, pulling the wagon.

The mules were valuable to my grandfather and served a vital role for him. My grandfather gave each of the mules a name. I remember Bill and Ed. My grandfather took care of and provided for the needs of the mules. He fed them, gave them water, nursed their wounds, protected them from predators, and provided them with shelter from inclement weather. When my grandfather plowed the fields or completed some other task with the mules, they worked together to accomplish the task at hand.

The "mules riding in the wagon" analogy was born out of my observation and assessment of the state of the church. Growing up in rural northern Mississippi, "bench warmer" or "bench member" was used to describe the church members who attended worship services one to five times per month but were not involved in any ministry of the church. The "mules riding in the wagon" analogy does not imply the people in the pews are brute beasts of burden who should shut up and work. The analogy illustrates the importance and value of the people in the pews to the ministry of the church. The people in the pews have a role to fulfill in the ministry of the church. The ministry leaders and the people in the pews work together as a team so that the ministry of the church serves God to the best of its ability.

In my current context, the level of engagement amongst the church where I currently serve is less than full participation of the membership.[1] I define active ministry engagement as working or serving on at least one committee, auxiliary, or board in the church and consistently attend Bible Study or Sunday School. The thesis guiding this project is that prophetic preaching can help to move the people in the pews to increase their ministry engagement in the

---

[1] This paper draws upon and incorporates insights from the 2020-2023 reflection and integrative papers.

church. Prophetic preaching is bible-based proclamation in which the preacher speaks to the inadequacies and insufficiencies of the present leading to a hopeful, truthful, and redemptive future. Prophetic preaching is a God-given directive delivered through the mouth and full embodiment of the preacher. I have described the problem as too many mules riding in the wagon.

A mule is not a pet. A mule is not ridden recreationally. A mule is not used for sport. When a new convert accepts Jesus Christ as their Lord and Savior, the Holy Spirit begins working within them to put them to work for the furtherance of the spread of the gospel of Jesus Christ. Every believer becomes a worker in the body of Jesus Christ as a member of a local congregation.

There is neither an agreed upon nor a consensus of a single definition of prophetic preaching. The common thread in homiletics is that prophetic preaching involves social issues and injustices. The preacher is compelled or motivated to speak out on issues affecting the community and the church. Lenora Tisdale says it is a term that "is currently used in church circles in ways that can be confusing and even conflicting."[2] It is a term that is not easily defined. Tisdale defines prophetic preaching as "preaching that is cutting edge and future oriented (yet not future predicting), and that addresses public and social concerns."[3] According to Tisdale, John McClure seeks to bridge the old with the new and current societal condition. McClure

---

[2] Tisdale, Nora Tubbs, *Prophetic Preaching: A Pastoral Approach,* (Louisville, KY: Westminster John Knox Press, 2021), 3.
[3] Ibid., 3.

says prophetic preaching is "an imaginative reappropriation of traditional narratives and symbols for the purpose of critiquing a dangerous and unjust present situation and providing an alternative vision of God's future."[4] One function of prophetic preaching is to demand change boldly and confidently in the face of perceived injustices. Marvin McMickle's contribution to prophetic preaching is to say, "Prophetic preaching shifts the focus of a congregation from what is happening to them as a local church to what is happening to them as a part of society."[5] Another function of prophetic preaching is to confront those in authority serving as a voice for the voiceless.

This project defines prophetic preaching as a proclamation in which the preacher speaks to the inadequacies and insufficiencies of the present leading to a hopeful, truthful, and redemptive future based upon the Word of God. It expands the focus from social issues and injustices to including personal commitment and inclusion of the believer in accepting God's invitation to join God working towards the visionary future based upon the Word of God. Every believer has been endowed with a spiritual gift that fits perfectly within the local congregation that must be exercised synergistically. Prophetic preaching in this project includes the personal commitment to working within the local congregation to address social issues and injustices.

---

[4] Ibid., 8.
[5] McMickle, Marvin Andrew, *Where Have All the Prophets Gone? Reclaiming Prophetic Preaching in America,* (Cleveland, OH: Pilgrim Press, 2006), 2.

The project will address the lack of ministry engagement of the people of the pews and present a vision to the church of what full participation of its members would look like. Discipleship and spiritual gifts of the people in the pews will be significant variables in the success of the church's ministry. Discipleship provides the motivation and dedication to the ministry of the church. Spiritual gifts through the direction of the Holy Spirit ensure synergy in the participation of the people in the pews.

When the believer confesses his or her belief in Christ Jesus and develops a close, personal, intimate relationship with God, the Holy Spirit will direct them into an area of ministry to edify the body of Christ and to further advance the ministry of the church. When the believer confesses his or her belief in Christ Jesus, the Holy Spirit gives them a spiritual gift to evangelize the lost, to edify the body of Jesus Christ, to build up the church, and to serve the local congregation. The Apostle Paul writes in I Corinthians 12:7, "the manifestation of the Spirit is given to each one for the profit of all." He also writes in Romans 12:6, "having gifts differing according to the grace that is given to us." The Apostle Peter says in I Peter 4:10, "as each one has received a gift, minister it one to another as good stewards of the manifold grace of God." Every member of the local congregation has a role to play and a function to fulfil in the ministry of the local congregation. Spiritual gifts are meant to be shared. Spiritual gifts are not meant to be hoarded. All congregations may not have all spiritual gifts represented. However, all congregations have all the spiritual gifts it needs to fulfil its ministry. No one spiritual gift is more valuable than any other spiritual gift. The value of a spiritual gift within a congregation is dependent upon the needs of each local congregation.

By definition, a disciple is a student, learner, or pupil. It generally is understood to mean a follower of Jesus Christ. Biblically, the disciples of Jesus spent a lot of time watching him interact with admirers and detractors. They spent time observing his daily devotional practices, prayer life, and ministerial activities. Jesus taught his disciples. Before his Ascension, Jesus commanded his disciples to do what they had seen him do.

A disciple is a person who spends time learning, studying, copying, and imitating Jesus Christ to move from spiritual infancy to spiritual maturity. The disciples of today must spend time with Jesus Christ through the power of the Holy Spirit. To make disciples, the disciple must read, study, meditate upon, and apply the Word of God. To make disciples, the disciple must begin to act, behave, and embody Jesus Christ through the power of the Holy Spirit. The disciples of today have been given the same command as the biblical disciples. Jesus commands today's disciples to do what he has done.

Discipleship brings Heaven into the life of the believer by joining God in God's work. Discipleship brings Heaven into the life of the believer by allowing the Holy Spirit to work through us to become God's representative here on Earth. Discipleship brings us comfort in times of sadness and sorrow. Discipleship brings us peace in times of turmoil. Tony Evans defines disciple as a person who joins "that developmental process that progressively brings Christians from spiritual infancy to spiritual maturity so that they are then able to reproduce the process with someone else."[6] The last words Jesus Christ told his disciples in Matthew 28:19 was to "Go therefore and make disciples of all the nations." Before Jesus issued the command to make disciples to his disciples, he first taught them, performed miracles before them, gave them power to perform miracles, preached before them, prayed for them, and died for them. A disciple spends time with his or her teacher to learn from them. Disciples would spend so much time with their teacher that they would walk like the teacher, talk like the teacher, preach like the teacher, and behave like the teacher.

Discipleship in the church today may not be as easily understood or expressed as in biblical days but it is still necessary. Today's disciples seek opportunities to care for the poor, provide housing for the homeless, care for the sick, provide food and water to the hungry and thirsty, and preach the salvific work of Jesus Christ on the Cross. Most importantly, discipleship's central purpose and motivation is to serve God by serving humanity.

By contrast, church work is an activity that does not necessarily reflect a personal commitment to Jesus Christ in the life of the worker. Church workers do not have to be born again, be the member of a local congregation, nor saved by the salvific work of Jesus Christ on the Cross. Church workers do have to be endowed

---

[6] Evans, Tony, *Kingdom Disciples: Heaven's Representatives on Earth,* (Nashville, TN: Lifeway Press, 2018), 7.

with a spiritual gift from the Holy Spirit. Church workers do not have to have a desire to increase their understanding of biblical teachings. They are not always concerned with advancing the Kingdom of God. Their motives may be more self-serving than service oriented toward others.

The project seeks to increase ministry engagement of the people in the pews through their relationship with God based through Jesus Christ. Discipleship is a necessary component in the lives of the people in the pews. Discipleship creates a higher level of commitment and dedication to the ministry of the church than church work. The goal of discipleship is to please God.

One of the byproducts of true discipleship in the life of the believer is ministry engagement within the body of the church. Because of discipleship, the people in the pews will work together as one unit performing his or her functions through the guidance of the Holy Spirit. Church ministry engagement as a byproduct of discipleship leads to a long-term commitment seeking to serve God through serving God's people. The commitment will also extend beyond the walls of the church into the community seeking opportunities to change social injustices.

Several senior pastors were asked about the ministry engagement level of their local congregations. The denominations of the senior pastors were Baptist, Church of God in Christ, Covenant, Lutheran, Methodist, Non-denominational, and Presbyterian. The senior pastors were African American and Caucasian. The senior pastors were male and female. The churches were in Illinois, Minnesota, Mississippi, Tennessee, and Texas. The average percentage of membership engagement according to those senior pastors was thirty percent. Seventy percent of church members attend weekly worship services one to five times per month and are not connected to the local congregation in any other capacity. Seventy percent of church members are satisfied with having a godly religion but not a relationship with God.

Religion does not move beyond a superficial, casual, surface-level, and passing acquaintance. Religion may recognize the existence of a supreme, supernatural power as creator and rule of the universe. Tony Evans says, "religion without relationship won't count for much."[7] Religion may lead some people in the pews to participate in a pattern of organized and structured worship exercises. Religion on its own merits will not lead to a deep relationship with God. James 2:17 (NKJV) says, "Thus also faith by itself, if it does not have works, is dead." Religion may bring the believer into the sanctuary to witness worship practices, typically on Sunday morning. Relationship with God brings the believer into the presence of God every day of the week. Those in relationship with God seek to spend as much time as possible with God. Tony Evans also writes, "God wants to be first in your life as your King, but He wants His relationship with you to be the motivating factor for you as His kingdom disciple."[8] God does not take second place in the

---

[7] Evans, Tony, *Kingdom Disciples: Heaven's Representatives on Earth*, (Nashville, TN: LifeWay Press, 2008), 53.
[8] Ibid., 54.

life of the Christian believer. God desires to be first always. Even though God desires to be first in the life of the believer, he or she must choose to make God first in their life. God never forces Godself into the believer's life. When the believer places God first in his or her life, the believer has unfettered access to God's blessings, provisions, and guidance.

God does not need anyone to believe that God exists. God does not need any of God's creation to praise and worship God. God is God regardless of what God's creation thinks. God wants God's creation to trust God, to serve God, and to be in a right, perfect relationship with God. Redeemed believers should have a desire to become disciples of Jesus Christ to connect with God's desire for a close, intimate relationship. God created men and women in God's image as well as with a desire for interactive contact. The Holy Trinity is in relationship with each other. Each member of the Holy Trinity communicates with every other member of the Trinity. Tony Evans says, "If God designed us with a deep need and a deep desire for intimacy in our human relationships and if intimacy reflects Gods image in us, you can expect God to look for intimacy in His relationship with you."[9] A deep, intimate, close relationship with God and the believer means the believer spends so much time becoming acquainted with God that every aspect of their personal life is based on the teaching and preaching of the Word of God. Evans writes, "To truly know someone intimately involves

---

[9] Evans, *Kingdom Disciples: Heaven's Representatives on Earth*, 92.

engagement, interacting, and understanding that go above and beyond cognitive realities."[10] Intimate relationship with God involves the believer reading the Word of God, utilizing his or her spiritual gift in service of God's kingdom, and living their life in ways in complete fulfillment of biblical principles. A close, intimate, and personal relationship with God requires a daily devotion to spending quality time with God. Intimacy with God creates a desire within the heart to serve God, to please God, to exalt God, to magnify God, and to honor God. One of the ways an active, ministry engaged person in the pews serves, exalts, and honors God is by serving God's chosen people.

Religious practices with limited authority of God as the head of a person's life allows Satan to control and dictate the person's actions more easily. Evans says, "Religion without God as the absolute ruler and authority is no threat to Satan. Life that seeks its own decisions and will apart from God is religion."[11] Religion without discipleship allows a person in the pews to make excuses and justify their lack of ministry engagement. Some of the excuses religious people make are not enough time, distance to the church is prohibitive, and the church is not doing what the church needs to be doing. None of those excuses are adequate excuses for the lack of ministry engagement. Time is never an excuse. Allocation of time and prioritization may be the issue. People find the time to do what is important to them. Distance is also dismissed as an excuse. The

---

[10] Ibid., 90.

[11] Evans, Tony, *Kingdom Disciples: Heaven's Representatives on Earth*, 128.

physical locations of churches do not change very often. The church is usually in the same location as it was the first time the person visited. Churches typically do not change locations from one year to the next. Churches stay in the same location for decades or centuries.

The church is a local assembly of redeemed believers who follow Jesus the Christ as Lord and Savior. After his resurrection, Jesus commissioned each local congregation to make disciples, teach all nations what they have been taught. Additionally, the church has been called to address the social needs of the people they are attempting to minister. Many people in the church do not fully understand the role of the church. Those people will never fully understand the role of the church with part time, partial, little or no engagement in the ministry of the church. No one can work in that which they do not understand.

When God builds a stronger relationship with the believer, he or she develops a desire to serve God. The believer serves God by serving others. Jesus tells his disciples in Matthew 25:35-40 that they fed him, gave him drink, clothed him, visited him in prison, gave him shelter, and nursed him back to health. Jesus told his disciples they did all those things to him when they did it for the least in society. The primary concern[12] of the church is to make disciples, to teach, preach, and baptize the unsaved. The second concern of the church in ministry is to provide for the needs of the people and the community. The Holy Spirit leads, guides, and

---

[12] Evans, *Kingdom Disciples: Heaven's Representatives on Earth*, 37.

directs the ministry of church to serve God by serving the least of those.

The words Christian and disciple are often used interchangeably; however, they are not the same. All disciples are Christians, but all Christians are not disciples. Early biblical followers of Jesus Christ called themselves brothers, sisters, or saints. The term Christian was initially used as a term of insult, derision, and ridicule by the non-Christian community. By definition, a Christian is a person who believes in Jesus Christ or an adherent to the teachings of Jesus Christ. Eventually the early followers of Jesus, adopted the name Christian as a term of honor, pride, and nobility. The early followers of Jesus came to relish being called a Christian. Today the term seems to have lost some of its sense of honor, pride, and nobility. Today the word Christian has become equated with simply a Sunday morning churchgoer. The word Christian is often used so loosely the power, effectiveness, and nobility of the word has lost is significance. For some a sense of shame has been connected to the word Christian. Some do not want to be identified with Christianity because of the negative news, publicity, and headlines depicted in the media.

Modern day church scandals have been a contributor to some of the negative sentiments and ideas regarding Christianity. Believers who selectively heed to some Christian tenets while ignoring others also impede the correct understanding of the power of Christianity in the life of the believer. The plethora of religious denominations has diluted the power, effectiveness, and nobility of what it means to be a Christian and contributed to the negative connation of Christianity. In the United States the number of persons who identify as Christian has been on a steady decline for about the past fifty years. In the 1970 census, ninety percent of all American citizens identified as Christian. In the 2020 census, sixty-four percent of all American citizens identified as Christian[13]. At its current downward trajectory, the percentage will drop below fifty percent by the year 2070. According to the Pew Research Forum, church attendance, participation, and involvement peaked in the United States in the mid-1980s.[14] Christianity and engaging in church ministry is becoming less and less of a priority in the life of many believers. Many people in the pews are seemingly content with sporadic and intermittent attendance than with making a deliberate effort to move from new convert to disciple.

Church ministry engagement also must compete with outside secular activities held at the same time typically reserved for church related activities. Growing up in rural Mississippi in the late seventies to mid-eighties, Sundays and Wednesdays were reserved for church ministry events. There were no youth activities, no sporting events, and no society meetings conducted on those days. Sundays were particularly revered. Alcohol and cigarettes were not

---

[13] PRRI Staff, *2020 Census of American Religion, The*, July 8, 2020, accessed August 23, 2023, https://www.prri.org/research/2020-census-of-american-religion/.

[14] Lugo, Luis and Stencel, Sandra, *U.S. Religious Landscape Survey, Religious Beliefs and Practices: Diverse and Politically Relevant*, (Washington, D.C.: Pew Forum Web Publishing, 2008), 36.

sold on Sundays. Gas stations and some restaurants were the only businesses open on Sunday. The American society of today has chosen to regard Sunday as just another day of the week. Many Christians also see Sunday as just another day of the week. They do not see a need to devote the entire day in service of Jesus Christ. Weekly church attendance and ministry participation for some Christians has seemingly become optional.

The Oxford English Dictionary defines a disciple as a person who believes in and follows the teachings of a religious or political leader. The Nelson Illustrated King James Bible Dictionary defines a disciple as a student, learner, or pupil. Tony Evans defines a disciple as "a believer in Christ who takes part in the spiritual-developmental process of progressively learning to live all of life under the lordship of Jesus. The goal of kingdom disciples is to live transformed lives that transfer the values of the kingdom of God to earth so that they replicate themselves in the lives of others."[15] A disciple of Jesus Christ is a perpetual student. Disciples of Jesus Christ always seek to learn more, do more, and transform into the image of Jesus Christ. Disciples of Jesus Christ understand they will never learn or know everything there is to know about Jesus.

As recorded in Matthew 28:19-20 (RSV), Jesus told his disciples to "Go therefore and make disciples of all nations, baptizing them in the name of the Father and of the Son and of the Holy Spirit, teaching them to observe all that I have commanded

---

[15] Evans, *Kingdom Disciples: Heaven's Representatives on Earth*, 16.

you; and lo, I am with you always, to the close of the age." The beginning of Jesus' Great Commission to the disciples and today's church are action words. True disciples are made. Making disciples requires deliberate, intentional, and purposeful intent. Making disciples is not a casual, spontaneous, or fly-by-night activity. Converts to Christianity do not automatically become disciples over a prerequisite amount of time. Jesus told his disciples and the church of today to go and make. The disciples in Matthew 28 went as Jesus instructed them. The early church went as Jesus instructed them. The church of today has changed the go-and-make strategy to a wait-for-them-to-come strategy.

Jesus also commands his disciples to baptize all nations and then to teach them to observe all things Jesus commanded. Baptism is another deliberate, intentional act a new convert completes. Baptism is a symbolic act that indicates the convert's decision to unite with the church of Jesus Christ. Upon conversion the believer must continue to be taught the commandments of Jesus. The salvific work of Jesus Christ is available to everyone. Many persons still do not know or understand the salvific work of Jesus Christ on the cross. The church through all its members must tell the story of the death, burial, and resurrection of Jesus Christ for the sins of all believers. Tony Evans calls this the primary concern of the church and defines it as, "The primary concern of the church - from Genesis to Revelation - is the glory of God through the advancement of the kingdom."[16] If each member of the church invites, encourages, and ministers to one other person, the gospel of Jesus Christ would spread across the entire globe in never-before-seen evangelistic numbers. True Christian discipleship not only benefits the individual believer but the local congregation and the universal church of Jesus Christ. The Apostle Paul writes in Ephesians 4:15-16 (NKJV), "but, speaking the truth in love, may grow up in all things into Him who is the head--Christ--from whom the whole body, joined and knit together by what every joint supplies, according to the effective working by which every part does its share, causes growth of the body for the edifying of itself in love." Paul encouraged all believers in the church in Ephesus that true growth in Jesus only comes when all the commands of Jesus are followed. Jesus is the model for all disciples to emulate. Paul furthers his argument that the body of the Christian church and each local congregation function best when every member fulfils his or her function within the body. Each member of the church has a role to fulfil within that congregation. The local congregation will not function to its full capability if every member does not fulfil his or her role.

Expanding on Paul's argument in Ephesians 4, new converts who do not progress toward discipleship in unity with a local congregation risk living their life based upon their own idea of what is right and wrong. They will do what is right in their own mind.

---

[16] Evans, *Kingdom Disciples: Heaven's Representatives on Earth*, 37.

They will become more easily led astray and more susceptible to the tricks, schemes, and wiles of the devil. Discipleship creates community within the body. Discipleship creates security within the body. Discipleship creates accountability within the body. Discipleship creates fellowship within the body. Discipleship creates unity within the body of Jesus Christ.

Given this context, concern, and theory, I want to accomplish the task of inviting the people in the pews to increase their level of ministry engagement. Prophetic preaching will be one mechanism presented as a plan to accomplish this task. Prophetic preaching will speak to the people God's plan for the ministry of the church to go forth and the need for all members to become involved in the ministry. Prophetic preaching will highlight for the people in the pews God's desire for an intimate, deeper, closer relationship which will lead to increased engagement on the social, communal, and personal levels in the ministry of the church. This plan does not explore or investigate the reasons why preaching, prophetic or otherwise, has been ineffective in addressing the issue of declining ministry engagement in local congregations.

In the preaching moment God is speaking through the voice of the preacher. In the preaching moment God is taking the initiative to connect, present Godself to some, introduce Godself to others, build a stronger relationship, encourage those in need, and to illustrate God's goodness. The preaching moment is one way God utilizes to speak to God's creation to invite the people in the pews to join God in God's work. When God shows the church a problem that needs to be addressed, God expects the church to respond to the problem. The problem God is showing the church is that everyone in the church is not fulfilling his or her role in the church. The church is failing to fulfil its God given direction of the church.

The general style of the biblical prophets is to provide an encouraging word to those who are struggling through difficult circumstances. The general structure of the prophetic message was things are bad. They may become worse. Despite the difficult circumstances, keep the faith, hold on, and trust God. In the end, everything is going to be alright. All of us need a reminder that good always triumphs over evil. All of us need to be reminded that God will never leave us nor forsake us. All of us need a reminder that love always overcomes hate.

Prophetic preaching must be able to speak with the boldness, power, conviction, and confidence to which they have been called. When an issue is revealed to the preacher by God, he or she must spend time with God contemplating and meditating on how best to speak on the topic to the people in the pews. The biblical prophets spoke to the people the words of God regardless of how the words would be received. According to McMickle, "With an urgency that could not be contained and a fervor that could not be controlled, the prophets declared 'Thus says the Lord' despite the ridicule, rebuke, and outright rejection that most of them experienced throughout their lives."[17] While this project does not investigate the reasons

---

[17] McMickle, Marvin Andrew, *Where Have All the Prophets Gone? Reclaiming Prophetic Preaching in America,* (Cleveland, OH: Pilgrim Press, 2006), 3.

why, the substance of most of today's preaching does not contain the same fervor or urgency. Many preachers avoid controversial topics, difficult texts, political issues, topics of racial equality, and current events. Many preachers spend more time ensuring all-inclusive language for God rather than speaking what thus says the Lord. Many preachers would rather preach sermons with no biblical content to appease the people in the pews than to risk the criticism of those persons. McMickle writes, many preachers "will preach with no particular urgency or attention paid to the prophets because no such urgency was laid upon them when they sat in our classes in Bible, theology, ethics, or even homiletics!"[18] Many preachers in today's pulpit choose not to offend or alienate the people in the pews at the expense of proclaiming the word of God as they know it to be.

In one of my summer residency classes, I asked my classmates if any of them said anything during their sermon on any of the following shootings: Sandy Hook elementary school in Connecticut, Pulse Night Club in Florida, Harvest Music Festival in Nevada, and the George Floyd murder in Minnesota. I was surprised and appalled at the number of my classmates who chose not to address any of those shootings in their respective pulpits. As preachers and pastors we cannot remain silent on some issues of national or international importance. We are compelled to speak a word from the Lord. I then asked a follow-up question asking how often we preach against social injustices: racism, sexism, educational disparities, wage

---

[18] Ibid., 7.

inequalities, gun violence, housing inequities, elder care, prison reform, political disenfranchisement, and a host of others. Once again, as preachers and pastors we cannot remain silent. Prophetic preaching demands the preacher in the pulpit address all issues revealed to us by the Holy Spirit. Prophetic preaching proclaims hope based upon God's grace and the Word of God amid pain, grief, loss, hardships, struggles, and difficulties.

Prophetic preaching should be utilized to speak to all societal injustices and ills. This project utilizes prophetic preaching to address the issue of declining ministry engagement amongst the people in the pews. Prophetic preaching identifies and presents the problem to the congregation. Prophetic preaching presents discipleship as a viable solution to reversing the downward trend of declining ministry engagement.

Chapter Two

Ministry Context

The four churches that provided the impetus for the development of this direction are Zion Springs Missionary Baptist Church, Okolona, MS, New Hebron Missionary Baptist Church, Aberdeen, MS, Pilgrim Baptist Church, St. Paul, MN, and New Bethel Baptist Church, Manly, IA. Pilgrim Baptist Church is where this project was created and served as the host congregation for project analysis and implementation. Zion Springs and New Hebron are African American churches located in rural northern Mississippi. Both churches were founded in the latter half of the nineteenth century. Zion Springs and New Hebron have a similar history, mission, ministry setting, and congregational socioeconomic status. Pilgrim is a multi-racial, multi-generational congregation located in a large metropolitan city. New Bethel is a small multi-racial congregation located in northern rural Iowa. All four churches share a common theological hermeneutic. They see the Bible as the Word of God and interpret it literally. They interpret the Bible through exegesis exclusively and apply a more literal interpretation to the written

Word.

Zion Springs and New Hebron were instrumental in my early childhood development. Because of their previous support I wanted to include them and have them share in my continuing spiritual and ministerial education pursuits of the Doctor of Ministry in Preaching degree at Garrett Evangelical Theological Seminary, Evanston, IL. Both churches supported me emotionally and financially when I graduated high school, attended, and graduated from college. Both churches contributed and participated in my development from my youth growing up in the church, to supporting me through my undergraduate college pursuits, and throughout my spiritual growth and ministry as a preacher and pastor. Both churches were invested in my completion of the Master of Divinity degree at Luther Seminary, St. Paul, MN.

Pilgrim Baptist Church (St. Paul, MN)

Pilgrim Baptist Church, St. Paul, MN, founded in 1866, is the second oldest African American church in Minnesota and the oldest African American church in the Twin Cities metropolitan area. Pilgrim has called twenty-four different senior pastors to serve the congregation. The founding members of the congregation were former slaves from Boone County, MO, who sailed up the Mississippi River and moved to St. Paul, MN, in 1863.[19] Upon arrival in the city of St. Paul, city leaders did not want all the former

---

[19] Pilgrim Baptist Church, http://www.pilgrimbaptistchurch.org/history/, accessed on September 28, 2023.

slaves to remain in St. Paul. The group was divided by city leaders. Half of the group was relocated about 150 miles north to the city of Duluth, MN, and half of the group remained in St. Paul.

Pilgrim Baptist Church is a multi-generational, multi-cultural church located in an urban, metropolitan, capital city of St. Paul. Pilgrim is located near the downtown area of St. Paul, MN, about two miles from the State Capitol Building. According to the United States Census Bureau, in 2021 the total population in St. Paul was 303,160.[20] The median age of the city is thirty-four.

Pilgrim currently has three hundred members with an average weekly attendance of seventy-five attendees to in-person worship. Its two oldest members celebrated their one hundredth birthday earlier this year. Two hundred of its members are over the age of sixty-five. There are twenty-five young people under the age of seventeen. The income levels of its members spans a wide range. Twenty percent of its members earn minimum wage or less. Ten percent of its members earn over $250,000 per year. Ninety percent of its members graduated from high school. Sixty-five percent of its members possess a bachelor's degree or postgraduate degree. Pilgrim's membership is ninety-seven percent African American. Three percent are White.

Pilgrim Baptist Church has a rich history in the state of Minnesota. The congregation played a prominent role in the civil

---

[20] "St. Paul, MN," United States Census Bureau, https://data.census.gov/table?q=st.+paul+mn&g=860XX00US55104, accessed September 28, 2023.

rights movement of the state and nation in the 1960s. Pilgrim has a strong history of being politically active. Some of its members have served on the city council and state legislature. St. Paul's current mayor, Melvin Carter III, is a former member of Pilgrim. In 1973 Pilgrim Baptist Church built and organized the Benjamin E. Mays Learning Center as a magnet school for ages kindergarten up to fifth grade. In 1986 the school was incorporated into the St. Paul Public School district and reinstituted as Maxfield Elementary School. Maxfield currently serves about 320 students in grades Pre-K through fifth. In 1971 Pilgrim built and operated an apartment complex located across the street from the sanctuary. Pilgrim built the complex to address the need for affordable housing in the community.

About three years ago Pilgrim decided as a church body to increase church membership. Church attendance and membership has been declining for over twenty-five years. The church body voted and decided to conduct a massive membership drive. The total current membership is about three hundred with about seventy-five weekly attendees for in-person worship. The pastor created a plan for the church to increase membership. He decided to invite all members to attend a Saturday morning workshop to present some evangelizing strategies. Out of three hundred total members with seventy-five in-person worship attendees, only fourteen people attended the workshop. Eight out of the fourteen people were ordained clergy. The pandemic shutdown postponed full implementation of the membership initiative and thwarted any meaningful results. When the church re-opened after the pandemic, the pastor decided to move forward and began implementing his initiative to increase the number of members in the church and to include more persons in the ministry of the church. The church did not follow his initiative, and no new members have been added as a direct result of the plan. Over the past five years, fifteen new members have joined the church with three joining through baptism by immersion.

The COVID-19 pandemic has had a drastically negative effect on the attendance of the youth and young adults in the church. Even though the church re-opened for in-person worship in June 2021, very few of the youth and young adult church members have returned. Twelve years ago, during one of its peak periods, the average weekly attendance to in-person worship was about five hundred people spread across two worship services each Sunday. The number of later evening worship services, concerts, plays, and celebrations has been curtailed.

Context Summary

The four churches included in my ministry context share common theological beliefs and styles of worship. The worship services consist of prayers, singing, offering, announcements, sermon, invitation to Christian discipleship, doxology, benediction. The sermon is the principal event of all their worship services. All preceding acts build toward the sermonic presentation. All post sermon events descend from the sermonic presentation. Singing also plays a critical role in the praise and worship experiences of all four congregations. Pilgrim has two organized choirs and a praise team group that maintain a rotating schedule each month. New Bethel does not have an organized choir and utilizes congregational singing only.

All four churches have the same Baptist theological beliefs, promote the same articles of the Baptist church, and prescribe to the Church Covenant of the Baptist Church.[21] They believe in the coexistence of the Holy Trinity. One God is represented in three persons, one Father, one Son, and one Spirit who are equal yet distinct. The Father, Son, and Holy Spirit are united to form the one God with unique roles and functions within the whole. The four churches believe the Bible is the authoritative, inerrant, and infallible Word of God. The Bible is written by at least forty different humans as inspired and under the direction of the Holy Spirit.

Pilgrim is a strong adherent to the autonomy of the local church. Each local church maintains the right to govern itself according to its own interpretation of the Bible. The local church can choose to be in relationship and fellowship with other congregations as part of an ecclesial body. However, the local congregation is not beholden to follow the decisions and practices of that ecclesial body.

Pilgrim believes in the priesthood of all believers. Priesthood allows each believer to minister to one another. Each believer is

---

[21] Boyd, R.H., *Articles of Faith and the Church Covenant*, (Nashville, TN: National Baptist Publishing Board, 2000), 5.

empowered to speak to God, read the Word of God, gifted by the Holy Spirit, and serve as messengers of the Holy God. Pilgrim celebrates the two ordinances of the church, baptism, and holy communion. It practices believer's baptism through total immersion. Immersive baptism is a symbolic representation of the death, burial, and resurrection of Jesus Christ. Believer's baptism replicates the form and subject of Jesus' baptism as recorded in Matthew 3:16, "When Jesus had been baptized, Jesus came up immediately from the water; and behold, the heavens were opened to Him, and He saw the Spirit of God descending like a dove and alighting upon Him." (NKJV).

The ordinance of communion or the Lord's Supper is a symbolic ritual instituted by Jesus before his crucifixion. The bread and wine consumed in communion symbolically represent the physical body and the shed blood of Jesus. All four churches believe all participants are commanded to always remember their eternal salvation is a gift to them from God through the sacrificial work of the Jesus Christ on the Cross.

In the four churches I have served and spent the most time serving and worshipping, I have had an up close and behind the scenes viewpoint of the operations of those churches. I have observed that about thirty percent and the same thirty percent of people are involved in the ministry of the church. The remaining seventy percent have a casual, part-time relationship with the church. For the church to fully accomplish its goals, all members of the church must work in synergy toward those goals. There must be a deliberate, concerted, and concentrated effort to invite the seventy percent to fulfill their ministerial role within the body. There must be an effort to identify the needs of the seventy percent of members who are not engaged in the ministry of the church. Once the need or needs of the seventy percent are identified, then a more concrete and deliberate plan must be created for the church to address those needs to encourage and invite them to become actively engaged. Preliminarily I have observed that the seventy percent may not feel they are part of the church and do not understand their role in the church. The seventy percent may not see ministry engagement as being a central component of their lives. The seventy percent may perceive the church as being too cliquish with too much nepotism.

Chapter Two

Homiletical Issue

The level of engagement amongst the current membership of many of today's churches is less than full participation. Prophetic preaching can be utilized to illustrate to the people in the pews the importance of their role in the church to increase their ministry engagement. When a new convert accepts Jesus Christ as their Lord and Savior, the Holy Spirit begins working within them to put them to work for the furtherance of the spread of the gospel of Jesus Christ. Every believer becomes a worker in the body of Jesus Christ as a member of a local congregation. When the believer confesses his or her belief in Christ Jesus and develops a close, personal, intimate relationship with God, the Holy Spirit will direct them into an area of ministry to edify the body of Christ and to further advance the ministry of the church.

Prophetic preaching proclaims the current situation directly. Prophetic preaching is ordained by God to proclaim the vision from God for how things should be. Prophetic preaching proclaims that all things will be made well but also proclaims it will not be achieved without a call to action. Prophetic preaching is a God-given directive delivered through the mouth of the preacher. The preacher in the pulpit must speak to the issues of why the ministry engagement is so low.

Gennifer Benjamin Brooks

Based upon my reading of Gennifer Brooks book, *Good News Preaching: Offering the Gospel in Every Sermon*, every sermon is an opportunity to proclaim the Goodness of God joyfully and energetically to all people in the pews. If the preacher in the pulpit is not excited, inspired, and believe in the sermon's message, the people in the pews might not be excited, inspired, and believe in the sermon's message. Brooks writes, "preacher and people become equal owners of the sermon, and this allows the good news of the sermon to relate equally to both preacher and hearers."[22] Good news is the sacrificial work of Jesus Christ on the cross. Because of the salvific work of Jesus on the cross, all persons can be delivered from the harsh penalties of sin and disobedience.

Gennifer Brooks believes that good news should be presented in all sermons. She further believes that many believers will turn deaf ears to preaching if an element of good news is consistently omitted. She writes, "The word "gospel," translated from a Greek word (*euangelion*), meaning good news, implies that the act of preaching is intended to offer good news to the hearers of the

---

[22] Brooks, Gennifer Benjamin, *Good News Preaching: Offering the Gospel in Every Sermon,* (Cleveland, OH: Pilgrim Press, 2009), 63.

preached word".[23] Brooks believes every sermon regardless of the chosen text offers an opportunity to positively present the gospel. She says, "the presence of explicit good news is an important element in every sermon and in every act of preaching as it enlivens, awakens, and energizes preacher and people for joyful living even in a troubled world."[24] The entire worship service should be a celebration of Good News. Effective preaching does not begin when the preacher stands behind the lectern and begins to speak. Effective preaching begins when the worship leader calls for the service to begin. Effective preaching allows all the preceding moments of the service to feed into the sermon's delivery, focus, and effectiveness. The preacher allows the Holy Spirit to use the prayers, songs, and testimonies to the build to an anticipatory receipt of what the Holy Spirit will speak to the people in the pews.

The grace of God presented in the sermon must be presented in ways the people in the pews can understand and accept. Not all sermon types and styles are applicable to all congregations. The content of all sermons will not be accepted or received by all congregations. The preacher must stay true to his or her calling and the deliver the message they received from God and rely upon the Holy Spirit to move in the hearts and minds of the people. Brooks says, "Contextualizing the sermon requires knowing the social, cultural, theological, and doctrinal norms as well as the experiences

---

[23] Ibid., xiii.
[24] Ibid., 5

of the community past and present."[25] My familiarity and comfort level with the people of the pews and the relationship I have with them in the churches where I have served allow me the freedom to speak freely, candidly, and openly. I am comfortable in making myself vulnerable in front of them and confident when I must speak in harsh tones with harsh language.

Brooks articulates that sermons should present the good news of the sacrificial work of Jesus Christ on the cross. Because of the sacrifice of Jesus Christ, everyone is afforded the opportunity for eternal salvation and to be delivered from the penalty of sin. Jesus paid it all for the repentant sinner. The primary focus of the church is to spread the good news and articulate the saving power of God's grace. My project strives to articulate the good news in God's plan for the believer to accept God's invitation to join in the work of the church. Every believer of Jesus Christ has a role to play in the life of the church. Every believer of Jesus Christ is given a spiritual gift to be used to edify the body of Christ and to evangelize the lost. God desires for every believer to join in the work of spreading the gospel of Jesus Christ. "Too Many Mules Riding in the Wagon" strives to invite, encourage, persuade, threaten, and guilt all hearers to join God in God's work to grow the body of Christ. That is good news.

"Too Many Mules Riding in the Wagon" will attempt to identify some of the reasons why people in the pews are apathetic and indifferent to actively engaging the in ministry of the church.

---

[25] Brooks, *Good News Preaching: Offering the Gospel in Every Sermon*, 59.

The preacher in the pulpit must make all efforts to fully understand the reasons to the best of his or her ability before developing and presenting a spiritual and theological foundation that speaks how and why those issues should be set aside and become involved in the ministry of the church. Brooks writes, "Preaching that is not contextual creates a void between preacher and people."[26] In addition to the reasons of the individual that were previously identified, the church is also culpable and bears some responsibility to the lack of ministry engagement amongst the people in the pews. The church must create an atmosphere where all people are valued, respected, and allowed to contribute. Preaching that addresses the issues that impedes ministry engagement must be mindful of the social, cultural, theological, and doctrinal norms present within the church and present a gospel message with good news.

Teresa L. Fry Brown

Teresa Brown's book, *Delivering the Sermon*, helped me to understand the importance of aural and oral presentation in sermonic delivery. The preacher must be aware of not only speaking the sermon but also mindful of how the sermon is heard. The sermon is the climatic conclusion of a praise and worship experience of all believers. All people play a role in that expression of praise. Worship service indicates how appreciative all persons are to what God has done, is doing, and will do. Brown writes, "Preaching is

---

[26] Brooks, *Good News Preaching: Offering the Gospel in Every Sermon*, 59.

worship and not a separate entity. The fully invested preacher understands that all elements of worship working together lead the congregation - and the preacher - into a deeper individual communal conversation with God."[27] Preaching plays a vital part in ushering the people in the pews to the communal conversation. The preacher spends time studying, reflecting, and meditating upon the Word of God to present God's message to God's people.

As a certified speech-language pathologist, Teresa Brown is skilled in the art of oral presentation and aural interpretation as it relates to sermon delivery. Brown believes a person's entire body is a tool to be used in presenting the gospel of Jesus Christ. She says the ear of the listener should be considered when preparing the sermon's message for delivery. She encourages the preacher to not only be cognizant of his or her voice. A preacher's body language delivers a message to the people in the pews along with the preacher's voice. Brown suggests six steps to delivering the sermon. She says the preacher should be "communicating the Word, enculturating the Word, voicing the Word, articulating the Word, embodying the Word, and animating the Word."[28]

Teresa Brown is correct in her suggestion to the preacher to use his or her body as a tool in presenting the gospel of Jesus Christ. The preacher should present the sermon's message to the people in the pews to the best of his or her ability. The voice is the primary tool

---

[27] Brown, Teresa L. Frye, *Delivering the Sermon: Voice, Body, and Animation in Proclamation,* (Minneapolis, MN: Fortress Press, 2008), 69.

[28] Brown, *Delivering the Sermon: Voice, Body, and Animation in Proclamation,* 4.

used in sermon deliveries by most preachers. In this sermon project, I will be more aware of my body language in presenting the message to the people in the pews. The preacher in the pulpit must be excited and believe in what he or she is preaching. His or her entire being must indicate their level of excitement. Brown writes, "Authentic preaching is to be conscious of one's unique preaching presence and use it fully as possible in proclaiming the gospel."[29] The preacher has the freedom to use all of his or her body parts to effectively and authentically preach the gospel. I also encourage the preacher to step outside their comfort zone but to not be someone or something they are not. The preacher must be aware of the fine line between authentic sermonic presentation and inauthentic performance. Preaching should not be seen solely as an entertainment performance. For the preacher, all oratorical endeavors are utilized for the sole purpose of presenting the gospel of Jesus Christ to the best of his or her abilities.

One of my biggest struggles as a preacher is assessing whether the message I intend to share is being heard and received. I am always mindful to preach and present the Word of God as accurately and truthfully as I believe and feel that it is. I believe most preachers have the same struggle. Brown writes, "In our desire to share the word of God, we must prepare to deliver the sermon so that it is palatable for others. The task is to deliver the sermon so that others

---

[29] Brown, *Delivering the Sermon: Voice, Body, and Animation in Proclamation*, 60.

can gain some spiritual weight."[30] As an African American preacher who formerly served as the senior pastor of a small, rural congregation in northern Iowa, I readily identify with and am familiar with the call and response preaching motif in African American worship experiences. Most of my sermons are more celebratory in style. However, in recent years I have pondered if this preaching style is the most effective in presenting the gospel of Jesus Christ to the world. There appears to be a less than enthusiastic response from the people in the pews to the preached word from the pulpit. The same preachers in the same pulpits are preaching to the same people in the pews. The preachers are preaching the same message and teaching the same lessons. Each Sunday there is the same lack of response and change in lives and behaviors.

Cleophus J. LaRue

Reading Cleophus LaRue's *Rethinking Celebration* impacted me to make sure the focus of my sermons is always God and what God has done, is doing, and will do. As an African American preacher, I am very familiar with the style of black preaching. One of my former pastors told me a few years ago that black preaching is an art form. For several years I have wondered if the call and response, emotive, celebratory style of African American preaching has become too performative. Larue says, "When evocative rhetoric becomes the be-all and end-all of preaching, performance reigns supreme, worship

---

[30] Brown, *Delivering the Sermon: Voice, Body, and Animation in Proclamation*, 86.

becomes a show, a congregation becomes an audience, and the preacher becomes a star performer."[31] Some preachers who practice this preaching style seem to place more emphasis on style instead of substance. Some preachers seemingly crave the post-sermon approvals and accolades of the crowd.

Cleophus LaRue wrote *Rethinking Celebration: From Rhetoric to Praise in African American Preaching* critiquing Frank Thomas' book, *They Like to Never Stop Praising God*. LaRue suggests a re-examining of Thomas' definition of celebration. LaRue says, "Thomas's definition of celebration is confusing at this point because he is not providing a theological definition of the term but merely describing when celebration happens."[32] Emotional celebration has been confused with effective preaching. Emotive congregational response has become the defining criteria of how good a sermon is. LaRue says, "A primary aim of an effective sermon is not merely to solicit an emotional response – even one that's put to good use – but rather to explicate the Scriptures with such clarity and insight as to make a claim on individuals when they hear the word of God proclaimed."[33] I have painfully sat through a lot of sermons from preachers who use a lot of words but say nothing. Another former pastor told me that you must preach first then whoop. LaRue argues, "This overemphasis on celebrating – especially for young black preachers – could be a deterrent to their

---

[31] LaRue, Cleophus J., *Rethinking Celebration*, (Louisville, KY: Westminster John Knox Press, 2016), 4.
[32] LaRue, *Rethinking Celebration*, 14.
[33] Ibid., 19.

development as sound biblical exegetes."[34] Whooping, to utter a loud cry or shout in expressing enthusiasm or excitement, is not a right but must be earned. My former pastor told me not to whoop if I have not preached.

In a direct criticism of Henry Mitchell and Frank Thomas, he says, "they have developed an affective (experiential) homiletic to which they have attached a cultural (festive) understanding of celebration, causing celebration to be understood primarily as a contrived rhetorical tool in the hands of a skillful preacher and responsive congregation as opposed to the spontaneous worshipful praise of God."[35] Many preachers have misinterpreted what Thomas said about celebration and have focused solely on the ending and not focused on the informational message that leads to an ending crescendo. This preaching project will not only articulate the issue in my ministerial context. The project will also define a working solution to address the issue identified. The project will take LaRue's advice by not only solely focusing on the sermon's culmination to invoke a response from the people in the pews.

There may be a perception amongst some congregants who feel they are on the outside of the congregation looking in waiting for an invitation to participate. Some people in the pews may feel they do not have time to be more engaged and involved in the daily ministry of the church. Some people in the pews may not know they have been gifted by the Holy Spirit to be a part of the ministry of the

---

[34] Ibid., 21.
[35] LaRue, *Rethinking Celebration*, 3.

church. Others may not know what the ministry of the church is or how they will fit into and help fulfil the mission of the church. The project will attempt to provide direction to how the church can move all the people in the pews to fully engage in the ministry of the church.

The sermons will attempt to end in a more celebratory style. The sermons will present to the people in the pews the impact and importance of the presence of God in their individual daily lives. The sermons will then expand to illustrate a daily relationship with God will extend to becoming involved in the ministry of the church. Cleophus LaRue says, "Church is more than a once-a-week encounter; it is an affirming presence that shapes and molds self-understanding, self-worth, behavior, and lifestyle."[36] Jesus taught his disciples in John 15:6 (NKJV), "I am the vine, you *are* the branches. He who abides in Me and I in him, bears much fruit; for without Me you can do nothing." In this illustration, Jesus teaches his disciples they must continue to remain connected to him to survive. Today's disciples must also remain connected to Jesus to survive. If a branch is cut off or separated from its vine, it will die. If any disciple is cut off or disconnected from Jesus, the disciple will no longer thrive or survive. Discipleship must be more than a once-a-week experience. Too many of today's disciples are attempting to survive and thrive with as little of a connection as possible to the Jesus the True Vine.

---

[36] LaRue, Cleophus J., *Heart of Black Preaching, The*, (Louisville, KY: Westminster John Knox Press, 2000), 24.

Marvin A. McMickle

The title of Marvin McMickle's book, *Where Have All the Prophets Gone? Reclaiming Prophetic Preaching in America,* captivated my attention and intrigued me as to what his reasons and motivations behind the question. Before reading his book, I imagined his assessment of preaching and preachers today would provide valuable insights to me and what I am attempting to explore. Marvin McMickle raises the question of whether true prophetic preaching is present in the church today. McMickle laments the lack of preaching that fails to truly address the issues plaguing the church. The modern-day preacher must address the issues that Jesus addresses with the same vigor and effort as Jesus. McMickle says, "Prophetic preaching moves a church from focusing on what is happening to them as a local congregation to what is happening to them as a part of the community at large."[37] He further encourages all preachers to preach using the same model as that of the biblical prophets. The Old Testament prophets preached with boldness, power, and under the unction of the Holy Spirit to directly address issues they felt were plaguing society.

The prophet's primary concern was to speak the word given to them by God. McMickle writes, "Prophetic preaching also never allows the community of faith to believe that participation in the rituals of religious life can ever be an adequate substitute for that

---

[37] McMickle, Marvin, *Where Have All the Prophets Gone: Reclaiming Prophetic Preaching in America,* (Holbrook, NY: Pilgrim Press, 2019), 2.

form of ministry that is designed to uplift the "least of these" in our world."[38] Furthermore, modern day preaching tends to avoid controversial topics such as politics, crime, racism, sexism, sexuality, justice, and righteousness. Many of today's sermons do not use the creative imagery utilized by the Old Testament prophets to adequately illustrate the ills plaguing the greater community. McMickle says, "our people will hear sermons about the values of patriotism, the paths to peace and prosperity, the appropriate methods for baptism and communion, why God does not approve of women in ministry and why a woman's right to control her reproductive choices is the single greatest evil in the world today."[39] Many of today's churches avoid the use of biblical texts that might confront and challenge the people in the pews to turn from their wicked, idolatrous ways. The Christians in today's churches excel in sending thoughts and prayers in the wake of tragedy but choose to ignore meaningful, practical solutions to address social injustice, biblical illiteracy, racism, sexism, crime, and gun violence.

Based on McMickle's suggestion, the lack of ministry engagement must be addressed directly, succinctly, and prophetically. Preaching must be one of the tools utilized to accurately define the current state of ministerial engagement. The Old Testament prophets serve as an excellent model for preaching to address lack of ministry engagement. They preached with boldness, power, and under the Unction of the Holy Spirit to directly

---

[38] Ibid., 3.
[39] Ibid., 7.

address the issues they felt were plaguing society. McMickle writes, "Part of prophetic preaching involves setting those teachings and commandments before God's people and challenging them to live those principles and practices in their daily lives."[40] He continues, "prophetic preaching is warning God's people of the consequences that can and may follow if they fail to or refuse to obey God."[41] God has given the church a command to spread the gospel of Jesus Christ. Every member of the church has a role to play to fulfil God's command. The church is failing to fulfill its God given command to go and tell the Good News of the salvific work of Jesus Christ on the cross. The church's ministry has shifted from going and telling to waiting for them to come.

Church attendance has been in a consistent and steady decline since the mid-1980's. In the United States, church ministry engagement peaked during the years 1984-1988 according to the Pew Research Center.[42] The church can no longer ignore the decline and hope the trend will reverse. The church must take deliberate, tangible, and fruitful action to reverse the trend. God has shown the problem to the church and God expects the church to solve the problem. The church must trust and believe that God has already provided them with all the tools and resources to solve the problem.

---

[40] McMickle, *Where Have All the Prophets Gone: Reclaiming Prophetic Preaching in America*, 54.

[41] Ibid., 54.

[42] Lugo, Luis and Stencel, Sandra, *U.S. Religious Landscape Survey, Religious Beliefs and Practices: Diverse and Politically Relevant*, (Washington, D.C.: Pew Forum Web Publishing, 2008), 36.

Before God calls and commands the church to do anything, God first equips the church. Luke 9:1-2 says, "Then he called his twelve disciples together, and gave them power and authority over all devils, and to cure diseases. And he sent them to preach the kingdom of God, and to heal the sick." (KJV) Jesus calls. Jesus gives. Jesus sends.

Frank A. Thomas

Frank Thomas highlights that African American preaching tends to end in an emotional praise celebration because it presents the pending deliverance of the downtrodden and oppressed by God. African American preaching should have a clear, implementable message before any emotional conclusion to the sermon. Prophetic preaching must have substance before style.

Frank Thomas writes, "the role of preaching is to attempt to over-record the tapes of fear, hatred, prejudice, unforgiveness, anxiety, and so on, and strengthen the tapes of hope, trust, love, forgiveness, and the like by reaching the core belief with the gospel."[43] Thomas continues, "the goal of the sermon was to demonstrate truth, illustrate truth, logically deduce truth, and lead people to intellectually assent to truth."[44] African American preaching tends to follow the model of the biblical prophets. The prophets had a

---

[43] Thomas, Frank A., *They Like to Never Quit Praising God: The Role of Celebration in Preaching, Revised and Updated*, (Cleveland, OH: The Pilgrim Press, 2013), 24.
[44] Thomas, *They Like to Never Quit Praising God: The Role of Celebration in Preaching, Revised and Updated*, 20.

message from God. When those messages were negative depicting God's displeasure with God's chosen people, the prophets preached with power, boldness, and conviction regardless of how the message would be received. The prophets generally concluded their proclamations with a word from God on a more positive note. Thomas says, "The focus was not on cognitive explanations, but an experience of the transforming, sustaining, and saving power of God in the midst of suffering and evil."[45] Preachers preached about the power of God to make all things well. God sides with the oppressed, less fortunate, marginalized, and the poor. God redeems, rescues, restores, and makes all things well.

Thomas defines celebration "as the culmination of the sermonic design, where a moment is created in which the remembrance of a redemptive past and/or the conviction of a liberated future transforms the events immediately experienced."[46] I define celebration as an external expression of an internal remembrance of the goodness of God in the life of the believer. The Merriam-Webster dictionary define celebration as a public ceremony or festivity. The Holy Spirit brings to remembrance the goodness of God and all the God-given blessings, the believer responds to illustrate their joy, excitement, and appreciation. "Too Many Mules Riding in the Wagon" will invite the people in the pews to celebrate what God has done, is doing, and will do in the life of the church. The church has the power of the Holy Spirit. The church must move

---

[45] Ibid., 20.
[46] Ibid., 49.

out of the sanctuary into the streets and go door to door, one house at a time, and invite the outsider to join the church of Jesus Christ. The church must tell the story of what God has done for their salvation.

Leonora Tubbs Tisdale

Lenora Tisdale provides an attempt to include a diverse perspective and a more inclusive point of view relating to prophetic preaching. Tisdale begins by highlighting McMickle's assessment of the lack of prophetic preaching in the African American tradition. Tisdale defines McMickle's explanation for the contributions to the demise of prophetic preaching which she defines as,

1. an overzealous preoccupation with the place of praise in some churches and services of worship (which has resulted in pastors' downplaying or ignoring the pain and suffering in our world

2. a false and narrow view of patriotism (that has sometimes equated unqualified praise of country with love of country; and

3. a focus in preaching on personal enrichment themes or a prosperity gospel to the exclusion or detriment of the gospel's broader social justice claims.[47]

She expands his critique of African American preachers to include

---

[47] Tisdale, Nora Tubbs, Prophetic Preaching: A Pastoral Approach, (Louisville, KY: Westminster John Knox Press, 2021), 1.

mainline denominational preachers. In addition to the definition of prophetic preaching as proposed by several theologians, she sees prophetic preaching as "cutting edge and future oriented (yet not future predicting), and that addresses public and social concerns."[48] Instead of providing a singular definition of prophetic preaching, she identifies seven hallmarks that make preaching prophetic.

1. Prophetic preaching is rooted in the biblical witness: both in the testimony of the Hebrew prophets of old and in the words and deeds of the prophet Jesus of Nazareth.

2. Prophetic preaching is countercultural and challenges the status quo.

3. Prophetic preaching is concerned with the evils and shortcomings of the present social order and is often more focused on corporate and public issues than on individual and personal concerns.

4. Prophetic preaching requires the preacher to name both what is not of God in the world (criticizing) and the new reality God will bring to pass in the future (energizing).

5. Prophetic preaching offers hope of a new day to come and the promise of liberation to God's oppressed people.

6. Prophetic preaching incites courage in its hearers and empowers them to work to change the social order.

7. Prophetic proclamation requires of the preacher a heart that breaks with the things that break God's heart; a passion for

---

[48] Tisdale, Prophetic Preaching: A Pastoral Approach, 3.

justice in the world; the imagination, conviction, and courage to speak words from God; humility and honesty in the preaching moment; and a strong reliance on the presence and power of the Holy Spirit.[49]

Tisdale's first and fourth hallmark resonate with me on what I propose to investigate. She also highlights prophetic preaching that presents liberation to God's oppressed people. She writes, "This world of ours desperately needs hope, and prophets are uniquely equipped by God to bring it."[50] Furthermore, prophetic preaching incites the hearer to work to change the social order. Most importantly Tubbs calls prophets the "harbingers of hope"[51] who can build bridges between congregational history and congregational mission. Tisdale also says about prophets, "In the midst of the lies and half-truths and doublespeak that are prevalent in our culture, prophets speak truth."[52] Prophetic preachers of today must speak to the recognized needs in ways to facilitate a change for a better and brighter future. Many of today's churches are navigating difficult challenges. They cannot maintain the status quo. Circumstances will not allow them to do what it has always done.

Prophetic preaching is required to speak to the issue that is prohibiting the church from fulfilling its mission. Tisdale says, "Prophetic preaching is concerned with the evils and shortcomings

---

[49] Ibid., 10.
[50] Ibid., 105.
[51] Ibid., 1085.
[52] Tisdale, *Prophetic Preaching: A Pastoral Approach*, 25.

of the present social order and is often more focused on corporate and public issues than on individual and personal concerns."[53] She also writes, "Prophetic preaching requires the preacher to name both what is not in the world (criticizing) and the new reality God will bring to pass in the future (energizing)."[54] Churches are failing to completely do the work God has ordained for them to complete. They are not fulfilling the commission they have been commanded by God to fulfil.

Prophetic preaching will present to the people in the pews there is still time to reverse the negative, downward trend. Congregations today have the power within the four walls to invite more people in the pews to engage in the ministry of the church. They can remove the perception that the vocal, visible minority is the makeup of the church. They can include all members in the ministry of the church. All spiritual gifts can be utilized in the ministry of the church.

The Holy Spirit has been instrumental in directing my steps and, in the words of Tubbs, rekindled the fire within. The Holy Spirit will order my steps to preach prophetically on the issue facing the church. The church is facing an organizational crisis in fulfilling its mission and commission. The church cannot continue to allow the current state of the church to trend in its current direction. Church membership and engagement has been declining for the past forty years. Prophetic preaching is required to speak boldly without fear of reprisal to address the issue. Prophetic preaching as inspired by

---

[53] Ibid., 10.
[54] Ibid., 10.

the Holy Spirit is required for this project to accurately articulate the problem and to present steps that lead to a successful solution to the problem. "Too Many Mules Riding in the Wagon" utilizes prophetic preaching that will voice God's concern for the people, which voices God's promises to the people of God, and that illustrates God's new mercies and blessings for the church.

Prophetic preaching reveals to the people in the pews that the current state of the church is not too bleak. The current state of the church can be salvaged to become what God has ordained it to be. Religious abuse, clergy scandal, and theological differences are not major contributors to the decline of church attendance and ministry engagement.[55] People who either stop attending church regularly or who cease to be involved in church ministry are not agnostics, backsliders, or infidels. Most of them have become discouraged, disenfranchised, or disengaged. For many people in the pews, ministry engagement has become a suggestion or a good idea but not an integral part of their lives.

Prophetic preaching is needed to address each of the three preliminary reasons for the lack of ministry engagement by the people in the pews. The first reason for the lack of ministry engagement is that the leadership is not asking for new people to become involved. Leadership relies on the same people to perform the same tasks. Leadership must expand their pool of trusted

---

[55] Gecewicz, Claire, "*Key Takeaways About How Americans View the Sexual Abuse Scandal in the Catholic Church*," https://www.pewresearch.org/short-reads/2019/06/11/key-takeaways-about-how-americans-view-the-sexual-abuse-scandal-in-the-catholic-church/, June 11, 2019, assessed on October 5, 2023.

members. Secondly, there is also a perception that exists among the people in the pews that there is a small clique of ministry participants. There does not appear to be a spirit of inclusion and invitation.

Thirdly, the most senior members of the church and ministerial team want assimilation and integration. They want all new people to do things the same way that they have always been done. The most senior members of the ministry team do not want to move beyond their comfort zone. They have an adverse reaction to change and trying new methods and methodologies. They seem to want change if everything stays the same. Similarly, the people in the pews do not want to learn the systems, reasoning, and ways of the existing operations before wanting to usher in change.

Prophetic preaching speaks a word from God to the people of God. Prophetic preaching addresses the problematic current state of what is with a conclusive message of divinely inspired word of deliverance to what is to be. Prophetic preaching may say that things are currently bad but also says that a better and brighter day is coming. Prophetic preaching also contains an element of pastoral care. The preacher in the pulpit recognizes a need or an issue in the local congregation and speaks to it. Leonara Tisdale's provides an approach to pastoral leadership. The approach recognizes every person's role in the body of the church and invites all people to become actively engaged in the ministry of the church. Tisdale's pastoral approach also addresses the misperception of the belief amongst the people in the pews that the church is made up of a small number of cliques and ministry workers. Marvin McMickle's desire for preachers to address injustice issues that exist amongst the pews will benefit the effort to increase Pilgrim's ministry engagement. If the church is to fulfil its mission and responsibility to address societal injustices, every gift of the Holy Spirit present amongst the church members is required.

Cleophus LaRue's approach to preaching presents a good method to deal with the potential change that may need to be made to bring new members into the church. Generally, people are not very receptive to change. LaRue's model for preaching to present a clear, coherent, and reasoned message to the people would have to be implemented to present a potential paradigm shift in the church. Great care must be taken and there is a fine line that must be navigated. New members can highlight some practices in the church that should be examined and possibly eliminated. However, the overall mission, goals, and purposes of the church can never be sacrificed.

Chapter Four

Expanding the Issue Beyond Homiletics

Prophetic preaching is a powerful tool that will invite the people in the pews to join God in God's work. Prophetic preaching will encourage all the members to unite with each other, to do their best to serve the Lord, and to invite all to join in the work of the church. Prophetic preaching will encourage the people in the pews to become the church God called it to be where the walk of faith transforms lives. God has already promised that when we seek first the kingdom of God and God's righteousness; and all these things will be added. (see Matthew 6:33). True discipleship is never content with their knowledge or relationship with Jesus Christ. True discipleship is constantly and perpetually seeking to know more of and more from God.

An authentically serious attempt must be made to invite the people in the pews to become the son or daughter God called and created them to be. God has a plan for the life of every believer of Jesus Christ. God is still inviting every person to become a disciple and to follow Jesus Christ. Every person was created by God for a purpose to serve God. Fulfilling God's purpose in the life of the disciple is born out of the disciple's relationship with God. Because of whom God is, what God has done, and the relationship God desires to have, disciples of Jesus Christ will do what God calls them to do to best of their ability.

Luke is the only gospel writer to record Jesus' Parable of the Barren Fig Tree in 13:6-9 (KJV) which reads:

> He spake also this parable; A certain *man* had a fig tree planted in his vineyard; and he came and sought fruit thereon, and found none. Then said he unto the dresser of his vineyard, Behold, these three years I come seeking fruit on this fig tree, and find none: cut it down; why cumbereth it the ground? And he answering said unto him, Lord, let it alone this year also, till I shall dig about it, and dung *it*: And if it bear fruit, *well*: and if not, *then* after that thou shalt cut it down.

When Jesus told the parable, the fig tree symbolized the children of Israel. In this parable, Jesus illustrates three basic principles of God's judgement. The first basic principle is that God places the elements of fruit producing in God's Creation. God expects fruit to be produced. The second basic principle is that God looks for fruit at the time of fruit harvesting. The third basic principle is that there will be a day of reckoning when everyone must stand before God and account for their actions. Most importantly, Jesus also illustrates God's extended mercy towards Israel. God's judgement, represented by the certain man, called for the barren fig tree to be cut down. God's grace and mercy, represented by the vinedresser, interceded, and gave the fig tree more time to produce and complete what God created it to produce.

In today's context, I interpret the fig tree to represent the church. Personally, the fig tree represents every Christian believer. The first lesson to be learned from the parable is God has the right to expect the church and the believer to produce what God created them to produce. Secondly, God nurtures and equips the believer to produce what God created them to produce. Thirdly, God gives an adequate amount of time for the believer to produce what God created them to produce. God does not leave the church or individual believer to fend for himself or herself. God takes an active role in developing the believer. Every Christian believer must join God in the development process which will lead to the believer becoming a disciple of Jesus Christ. The preacher in the pulpit must deliver the message of the salvific work of Jesus Christ on the Cross so that the people in the pews will learn and understand what God has done, is doing, and will do for the believer to accept God's invitation to discipleship.

By definition, a disciple is a student, pupil, or learner. In the New Testament, the word is most associated with the twelve named disciples of Jesus Christ as recorded in Matthew 10:1-4. The word disciple is only used once in the English translation of the Old Testament in Isaiah 8:16. Isaiah refers to disciples as someone who is taught or instructed.

Disciples of Jesus Christ are led by Jesus Christ and follow the teachings and instructions of Jesus Christ. Disciples of Jesus Christ are taught to become disciples. Making disciples is more than just showing reverence to the Risen Savior. Making disciples is one of the signs that point to the certainty of the resurrection of Jesus Christ. When the church and all its believers actively participate in the Great Commission of the church, it is proof that Jesus Christ is alive and seated at the right hand of God. Fulfilling the Great Commission proves Jesus gave the command, the Holy Spirit filled the church, and the church heard the voice of God.

Gabi Markusse

Discipleship is an impossible demand if left to the believer's skills and abilities alone. True discipleship can only be achieved through the indwelling of the Holy Spirit. When Jesus made the demand for the disciples to take up their cross and follow him, Jesus intended for them to stay connected and in contact with him to be successful. In *Salvation in the Gospel of Mark: The Death of Jesus and the Path of Discipleship,* Gabi Markusse highlights the failures of the twelve named disciples in Mark's gospel to follow Jesus. She uses how the disciples desert Jesus when He is arrested in the Garden of Gethsemane as an example to prove her point. She also references Peter's denial knowing Jesus at his trial as another example of the disciples' failure.

The disciples' failure to remain true in their calling to follow Jesus was due to them relying on their own strength. Markusse writes, "Those seeking to obey God, and be a part of his Kingdom, will need to follow Jesus unto death, looking to please God rather than themselves. This is not possible to do as a human. However, with the Holy Spirit, in whom the one seeking repentance is baptized through the death of Jesus, it is made possible."[56] All believers must learn from the failures of the biblical disciples. The believers of today must rely on the Holy Spirit to become and grow into mature discipleship.

While the disciples of today may not be faced with the same challenges as the Markan disciples, they will face challenges. Some of today's challenges that believers face is work-life balance, income maximization, racial disparity, gender inequities, and socio-economic gaps. Jesus rhetorically asked the disciples in Mark 8:36-37 (KJV), "For what shall it profit a man, if he shall gain the whole world, and lose his own soul? Or what shall a man give in exchange for his soul." However, Markusse says, "within each person, God's will is chosen above one's own will."[57] Despite the demands and challenges of discipleship, Jesus expects all of his disciples to commit to be the best student and follower under the guidance of the Holy Spirit. Jesus expects every believer to fulfil his or her role as the church's strives to fulfil the Great Commission.

Even though the disciples struggled at times to be the follower Jesus invited them to be, they were ultimately successful in doing

---

[56] Markusse, Gabi, foreword by Paul Middleton, *Salvation in the Gospel of Mark: The Death of Jesus and the Path of Discipleship*, (Eugene, OR: Pickwick Publications, 2018), 65.
[57] Ibid., 178.

what Jesus called them to do. The last verse in Mark's gospel says "And they went forth, and preached every where, the Lord working with them, and confirming the word with signs following. Amen." (KJV) The disciples did what they could to the best of their ability. After the ascension of Jesus Christ, the Holy Spirit worked through the disciples to prove the power of God, and the calling God placed upon their lives. Despite the failure of the nine disciples in casting out a demon in Matthew 17, Jesus continued to give them miracle-working power in Luke 9:1-2. Peter did deny knowing Jesus, yet he was forgiven and became the de facto leader of the newly ordained apostles. The disciples did desert Jesus in the Garden of Gethsemane, yet they did become great evangelists in spreading the gospel of Jesus Christ. Markusse posits the disciples' early failure and ultimate success serves as an example for today's believer. She writes,

> When interpreted together with the demands of discipleship and the promise of restoration in 14:28 and 16:7, their failure either provides Mark's audience with hope that they may one day also overcome their failures and be welcomed back as followers of Jesus, or at least that they may find comfort in that Jesus's first followers were also not able to follow flawlessly.[58]

Christian discipleship may not be easy, but it is rewarding and enriching. Not only does Christian discipleship bless those to whom

---

[58] Markusse, *Salvation in the Gospel of Mark: The Death of Jesus and the Path of Discipleship*, 50.

we are ministering, it also blesses those who are ministering. The believer serves God by serving others.

Markusse believes that the call of the twelve named disciples by Jesus Christ was an impossible task according to the Gospel of Mark. The call proved to be impossible because they could not have accomplished it on their own. According to Markusse, Mark's gospel records the humanly failures of the disciples. Mark's gospel records Peter's denial (Mark 14:66-72), Judas' betrayal (Mark 14:10-11), the failure of the disciples to cast out a demon (Mark 9:14-20), and the disciples abandoned Jesus in the Garden of Gethsemane (Mark 14:50). The gospel also records the commitment and dedication that Jesus expects of his disciples in Mark 8:34 (KJV), "Whosoever will come after me, let him deny himself, and take up his cross, and follow me." Jesus desires that he plays the preeminent role in the lives of all his disciples. Discipleship also may prove to be burdensome. Regardless of the difficulties, challenges, and burdens, Jesus still desires and expects his disciples to follow him.

Markusse's work and study provides an importance nuisance of understanding to me and my project. When a non-believer becomes a new convert and then moves to a disciple, he or she needs to understand what they are going into to the best of their ability. When the people in the pews decide to accept God's invitation, there will be challenges, difficulties, hardships, and burdens, but rewards at the same time. It is a blessing to be used by God. A sense of service and fulfillment is felt when God uses a disciple of Jesus Christ to spread the gospel of Jesus Christ. Left to our own skills, talents, and abilities, discipleship is impossible, and failure is eminent. With the Holy Spirit working in us and through us, the challenges, difficulties, and burdens can be overcome. Mark's gospel concludes, "And they went forth, and preached every where, the Lord working with *them*, and confirming the word with signs following." (Mark 16:20, KJV).

As a disciple of Jesus Christ, I desire to have a close, intimate, and personal relationship with God. I want everything I do to be pleasing in God's sight. I want to successfully complete everything God has called me to do. The Bible is one of the main tools at my disposal I use to cultivate my relationship with God. The Bible is the Word of God and the first consultant I rely on to understand and know God. I compare all theological and homiletical thoughts, ideas, and arguments with God's Word, the Bible.

Cedric E.W. Vine

When Jesus gave the disciples the Great Commission recorded in Matthew 28, Jesus was not enacting a ministry to increase the number of people in the pews on Sunday morning. Jesus was not creating an initiative to increase the amount of money collected on a weekly basis. Jesus was not creating a competition amongst local pastors for weekly television broadcasts. The focus of the Great Commission is to transform all of humankind through the acceptance of Jesus Christ as Sovereign Lord and Risen King. Jesus desires for all nations to follow Him as their Savior.

In *Jesus and the Nations: Discipleship and Mission in the Gospel of Matthew,* Cedric E.W. Vine suggests the Great Commission is deeper than a simple invitation to duplicate or imitate the life of Jesus Christ. Vine identifies five roles found in Matthew's gospel: "prophets, righteous persons, disciples, wise men, and scribes."[59] Vine also defines the "idealized disciple."[60] Of the idealized disciple, Vine says, "In the ancient world students learned through comprehending a teacher's words and imitating his deeds."[61] Imitation of a teacher in the ancient world was much easier than it is for a student in today's context. Disciples of Jesus face many competing interests that the ancient disciples were not confronted by.

Vine proposes an understanding of the Matthean narrative and understanding of discipleship that contains limitations for today's disciples. Vine suggests the idealized disciple may not be possible in today's context. Vine says there are "limitations to imitation" that the modern disciple face which make complete imitation impossible to achieve.[62] Vine says the first limitation, "an implicit limitation results from the tension between Jesus's emphasis on correcting your inner world and the fact that the reader is virtually never allowed into the inner world of Jesus's own thoughts."[63] Having the

---

[59] Vine, Cedric E.W., *Jesus and the Nations: Discipleship and Mission in the Gospel of Matthew,* (Eugene, OR: Pickwick Publications, 2022), 6.

[60] Ibid., 6.

[61] Ibid., 6.

[62] Vine, *Jesus and the Nations: Discipleship and Mission in the Gospel of Matthew,* 91.

[63] Ibid., 93.

mind of Christ may be difficult but not impossible. Having the mind of Christ means the believer should do what Jesus did. Jesus surrounded himself with men and women who had the same beliefs, ideas, and thoughts of what the ideal life should be. Jesus surrounded himself with men and women who were striving to have as close of a relationship with God as possible. Jesus surrounded himself with men and women who were willing to speak out against injustices, prejudices, and societal inequalities. Jesus also spent time in solitary prayer and meditation. Having the mind of Christ includes solitary time spent in prayer and meditation.

Just as today's disciples is limited in getting into the mind and inner world of Christ, the Bible is limited in recording the actual words of Christ. Vine writes, "A second limitation on the reader's ability to imitate Jesus relates to the restricted access to his words. Jesus obviously said more than is recorded in the Gospel."[64] John's gospel ends with the clarifying statement on the select transcription of the words of Jesus in 21:25 (KJV), "And there are many other things which Jesus did, the which, if they should be written every one, I suppose that even the world itself could not contain the books that should be written." Even though the Bible is a limited recording of the life of Jesus Christ and God's relationship with God's creation, the true disciple must use it as his or her foundation to accept God's invitation for an intimate, close relationship with God.

Because of the limitations of imitation facing the modern-day

---

[64] Ibid., 93.

disciple, becoming the idealized and model disciple becomes unlikely. Vine says, "The challenge that this picture of discipleship presents is that it requires far more interpersonal contact than industrial or postindustrial societies typically permit. Extended working hours, two-income households, multiple career changes, and nuclear families, all put pressure on interpersonal relationships and leave little time to invest in others."[65] Despite the challenges Jesus expects his disciples to follow him, teach all nations, and baptize in the name of the Lord.

Jesus understands the challenges his disciples face. Jesus faced some of the same challenges in his earthly ministry that his disciples have faced and will face. Jesus faced the challenge of poverty (Luke 9:58), experienced exhaustion (John 4:6), was betrayed and denied by personal friends (Matthew 26:47-56, 69-75), and experienced sorrow and disappointment (Luke 19:41). He also was tempted by Satan (Matthew 4:1-11) and felt forsaken by God (Matthew 27:46). Jesus suffered from the pangs of rejection and disbelief of his ministry (John 7:5; Luke 4:29-30).

Despite the challenges of his earthly ministry and the limitations of imitation, Jesus desires for his disciples to invite all nations to accept Jesus Christ as their Lord and Savior. Jesus did not force anyone to follow him during his earthly ministry. Jesus does not force anyone to follow him today. Jesus does not want his disciples to use force in their evangelistic efforts. Vine writes,

---

[65] Vine, *Jesus and the Nations: Discipleship and Mission in the Gospel of Matthew*, 95.

"instead of a law-abiding faithful generation driving out before them the wicked inhabitants from the land of Canaan, Jesus desires that a faithful remnant of Israel encourage the nations to accept him as sovereign and to become law-observant members of his kingdom, all while retaining tenure of their own land."[66] The salvific work of Jesus Christ on the cross must be told so that all nations can be transformed to become God's chosen people.

Full participation is required for the local congregation to accomplish its God-given commission. Vine presents a modern understanding of the Great Commission recorded in Matthew's Gospel to all nations that accepts the kingship of Jesus Christ. Vine presents a missional understanding of the commission to the church that removes all natural boundaries and is not concerned with local church growth. Adding names to the church roster may be a byproduct of the Great Commission but it is never the end goal. Vine's defined discipleship roles serve to redirect the understanding of the Great Commission to be a kingdom building initiative with Jesus Christ as King instead of as a local church building initiative.

As previously stated, the Bible is my primary consultant in which to frame theological and homiletical arguments. I have stated previously that the local congregation is commanded to fulfil the Great Commission as recorded in Matthew 28:19-20. Vine's movement of the commission to a more missional construct provided a great lens in which I viewed this project.

---

[66] Vine, *Jesus and the Nations: Discipleship and Mission in the Gospel of Matthew*, 160.

Walter Brueggemann

One of the challenges and struggles I face as a preacher is whether or not the words I speak from the pulpit are resonating and impacting the people in the pews. I assume if the words I speak are biblically accurate, theologically sound, and Holy Spirit inspired then the people in the pews will immediately cease sinful activities and center their entire lives around the word of God. Sermon reactions are typically the same: head nods and smiles, "Amen," "preach, preacher," "Yes," and handclaps. Post sermon feedback usually consist of the following: "Great sermon," "I really enjoyed it," "Great job," and "Powerful word." However, the people in the pews seemingly make little change and seem to be just going through the motions repeating the same behavior and lifestyle choices.

Discipleship is not an initiative to adjust or manipulate the socioeconomic or financial statuses of a local congregation. In *Evangelism and Discipleship: The God Who Calls, The God Who Sends*, Walter Brueggemann argues that discipleship is a lifetime and life adjusting commitment. Brueggeman says, "Discipleship is not just a nice notion of church membership or church education; it entails a resituating of our lives."[67] Disciples of Jesus Christ seek to implement the teachings of Jesus into every aspect of their life. Disciples of Jesus Christ strive to emulate the words, teachings, and

---

[67] Cox, Meg E., editor, Walter Brueggeman, "Evangelism and Discipleship: The God Who Calls, The God Who Sends," *Cynicism and Hope: Reclaiming Discipleship in a Postdemocratic Society*, (Eugene, OR: Cascade Books, 2009), 230.

actions into every facet of their lives. Brueggemann says, "The disciple is the one closely associated with the master-teacher, a profoundly undemocratic notion, for the relation consists in yielding, submitting, and relinquishing oneself to the will of purpose of another."[68] God desires to use every believer in the work of spreading the salvific work of Jesus Christ to the entire world. To be used effectively, the believing disciple must orient his or her life to God's will. Disciples of Jesus invite others to share in the joy, grace, and mercy extended to them.

The people in the pews have fallen short and abdicated their discipleship responsibilities. Brueggemann says, "prophetic preaching is the enactment of hope in contexts of loss and grief."[69] Even though today's disciples have been lacking in effort, God still allows them another opportunity to join God in God's work. There is still time for the church to join God in creating the society God intended. Brueggeman continues and says prophetic preaching "attests to the power of YHWH to create new historical possibilities where there is no ground for expectation."[70] Pilgrim Baptist Church is in a seemingly impossible situation. God has already provided Pilgrim everything it needs to successfully evangelize and grow the body of Christ and the ministries of the church. God can work many miracles through the life of Pilgrim.

---

[68] Cox, *Evangelism and Discipleship: The God Who Calls, The God Who Sends*, 230.

[69] Brueggemann, Walter., *The Practice of Prophetic Imagination: Preaching an Emancipating Word*, (Minneapolis: Fortress Press, 2012), 110.

[70] Ibid., 11.

Humankind is caught between two seemingly opposed entities, the will of God and humanity's desire to live on this earth successfully. The people in the pews must navigate an earthly existence where the trappings of society create a spiritual dilemma. Brueggeman says prophetic proclamation "begins in wonder concerning the inexplicable abundance willed by God the creator."[71] Discipleship navigates earthly successes through the realities of Godly, church ministries. The disciple, working through the ministries of the local congregation, expresses his or her relationship with God through service on boards, auxiliaries, or committees. The disciple never loses sight of the wonder, power, and awesomeness of Almighty God.

Amid difficulties and setbacks, disciples of Jesus Christ always look for the promises of God to be fulfilled. Discipleship promotes, presents, and strives to create the perfect world God promises. Brueggeman writes, "Prophetic proclamation is an attempt to imagine the world as though YHWH-the creator of the world, the deliverer of Israel, the Father of our Lord Jesus Christ whom we Christians come to name as Father, Son and Spirit - were a real character and an effective agent in the world."[72] Disciples know the life-changing power of God. Disciples know what God has done in their lives. Disciples accept God's invitation to tell God's story and what God has done for them. Disciples desire for everyone to accept

---

[71] Ibid., 11.
[72] Brueggemann, *The Practice of Prophetic Imagination: Preaching an Emancipating Word*, 3.

God as their Lord and Savior and to join God's invitation to tell the salvific work of Jesus Christ on the cross.

Tony Evans

Tony Evans presents the primary concern of the church as to make disciples in his book, *Kingdom Disciples: Heaven's Representatives on Earth.* He argues that Jesus gave his disciples the Great Commission to spread the gospel of Jesus Christ to the entire world. The Great Commission now spreads to the modern-day church. All other societal issues are important to the church and the church needs to be involved and participate in those issues to facilitate a solution that will benefit all of society. Evans highlights that God still desires for all believers become disciples of Jesus Christ. He argues that accepting Jesus Christ as your Lord and personal Savior gains the believer citizenship into Heaven.[73] Becoming a disciple of Jesus Christ gets Heaven into the life of the believer here on Earth. New convert conversion and church membership is God's invitation to the believer for the believer to join God in God's work on Earth. The Holy Spirit gifts each believer to serve in the ministry of the church to spread the gospel of Jesus Christ.

This project was crafted and created because of my reading Tony Evans' *Kingdom Disciples: Heaven's Representatives on Earth* and teaching a Bible Study class based on his book. Evans writes, "You

---

[73] Evans, Tony, *Kingdom Disciples: Heaven's Representatives on Earth,* (Nashville, TN: Lifeway Press, 2018), 7.

must believe on the Lord Jesus Christ to go to heaven, but you must confess the Lord Jesus Christ with the content of your life to follow Him as a disciple."[74] Evans also referenced I John 4:14-15. Reading those two verses along with Evans statement on believing and confessing Jesus Christ as Lord spoke a new word to me as if the voice of God was whispering in my ear. I John 4:14 illustrates discipleship as the Word of God being received, witnessed, and then encouraged to testify. God reveals Godself to men and women. God speaks the Word of God to men and women. God then commands and expects men and women to tell what they have seen and heard. This verse opened my eyes to God and solidified God's plan for my life in ways I had not expected nor fathomed.

In I John 4:14, the Apostle John encourages Christians to tell God's story. He encourages them to become witnesses to what they have seen and heard God do and say in their personal lives. John assumes that God has been actively involved in the lives of his readers. John writes to invite all believers to join him in fulfilling the Great Commission of Jesus Christ recorded in Mathew 28:18-20 to make disciples, to teach all nations, and to baptize new converts in the name of the Father, Son, and Holy Spirit.

All confessed believers are called and expected to spread the gospel of Jesus Christ and witness to the miracle-working, saving power of God. The Holy Spirit equips all believers to witness for the Lord. The Holy Spirit uses the believer's voice to speak. The Holy

---

[74] Ibid., 78.

Spirit uses the believer's feet to walk. The Holy Spirit uses the believer's hands to work. The Holy Spirit uses the believer's legs to run. Oftentimes the Holy Spirit only needs the person in the pews to stand and be in the place. The Holy Spirit will take over after that.

There are diverse types of witnesses in the legal system that are similarly present in the Bible and in the church today. In the legal system, there are reluctant witnesses, hostile witnesses, expert witnesses, character witnesses, percipient witnesses, and eyewitnesses. The parents of the man who was born blind and healed by Jesus in John 9:13-27 are one example of a reluctant witness. Peter's denial of being a disciple of Jesus Christ is an example of a hostile witness in Mark 14:66-72. The apostle Paul in Philippians 3:4-8 is an example of an expert witness. The centurion at the cross for the crucifixion of Jesus Christ in Luke 23:47 is an example of a character witness. Mary Magdalene, Peter, and John arriving at the tomb after the resurrection of Jesus in John 20:1-9 are examples of percipient witnesses. John says in I John 4:14 that he was an eyewitness to the miracles, sermons, parables, crucifixion, resurrection, and ascension of Jesus Christ.

Most people will find themselves fluctuating from one witness type to another. The type of witness the believer embodies is dependent upon where the person is in his or her relationship with God, the events in the life of the witness, and the comfort level of the witness in witnessing. If the testimony of the believer is reluctant, hostile, or characterizing, the glory of God can come forth, shine, and be revealed. If the testimony of the believer is one of expertise or from a percipient's point of view, the glory of God can come forth, shine, and be revealed.

Conclusion

Many of today's churches have all the gifts, talents, skills, finances, personnel, and resources to accomplish what God has called it do. However, I am uncertain of its desire to implement the proposal that will be presented to them. There is a lot of talk in some constituent circles of a need to do something to reverse the negative trend. There has been little to no action taken to reverse the negative trend. The time has come for Pilgrim to stop talking about the problem and take action to solve the problem.

The structure of the messages of the Biblical prophets to God's chosen people was that things were bad. They may get worse. God is not pleased and will allow suffering to endure for a while but in the end, God will forgive, restore, redeem, and make everything alright. Because God will eventually make all things well, the believer should never lose hope, should always keep the faith, and through it all, should celebrate.

"Too Many Mules Riding in the Wagon" follows the model of the biblical prophets to reveal to the people in the pews the current level of church ministry engagement. The preaching project will prophetically declare that the current trend will continue to decline and degrade if drastic action is not taken. The preaching project will present to the people in the pews each member's role in the ministry of the church. Finally, the preaching project will present a climatic resolution to the issue the church is facing that will end with a prophetic declaration that all things will work together for good. All members of the church are expected to become engaged in the ministry and fulfil his or her role in the ministry of the church. to fulfil God's command. The church will function as a synergetic body representing the body of Jesus Christ. The Holy Spirit will lead and guide the church to preach the gospel of Jesus Christ, to baptize in the name of the Father, Son, and Holy Spirit, to be God's witnesses, representatives, and ambassadors on Central Avenue, St. Paul, Minneapolis, outstate Minnesota, Wisconsin, Iowa, Mexico, Canada, North America, South America, Europe, Asia, Africa, and the entire world. Pilgrim will one day be able to say as Jesus said, "It is finished." Pilgrim will say as Paul said, "We have fought a good fight. We have run the race. We have finished the course." The church will shout the victory and give God all the praise and honor God is due.

"Too Many Mules Riding in the Wagon" takes advantage of the freedom and connection I have built within my preaching context to speak a word from the Lord to address the issue I have observed plaguing the church. Because of the relationship between the two of us, I have the freedom and license to speak powerfully, forcefully, and prophetically to address the lack of ministry engagement by seventy percent of the church members.

Chapter Five

Project Plan and Process

The project plan developed and preached a series of prophetic sermons that invited the people in the pews to increase their ministry engagement in the church. The sermons presented to the people God's desire for the believer to serve God by serving God's people. The sermons first presented God's call of the individual to transition from a non-believer to a new convert and then to transition to a disciple. The sermons presented God's sending of the Holy Spirit to dwell in the life of the believer.

Upon the acceptance of Jesus Christ as Lord and Savior, the Holy Spirit then equips the people in the pews to recognize and understand their role in the ministry of the church. When each believer becomes a disciple and unites with a congregation of believers, God then calls the body of believers into a discipleship relationship as a community of servants and worshippers.

The Holy Spirit equips the people in the pews to work synergistically within the body of the church. The sermons presented to the people in the pews God's plan for every believer to provide witness of the Good News of Jesus Christ whenever, however, and to whomever the opportunity presents itself. For the church to fully accomplish its God given mandate, every member of the congregation must be actively engaged and working together in constructive collaboration to accomplish its mission.

Design and Implementation

My initial hypothesis about why seventy percent is not involved in the ministry of the church is they do not feel welcomed as part of the church. They possibly believe the church to be cliquish, and what they have to offer will not be accepted or received by the perceived powers that be. Secondly, seventy percent do not understand how their spiritual gift fits within the ministry of the church. They also do not understand what the first primary concern of the church is. Thirdly, seventy percent do not see ministry engagement as being a vital component of their lives. They are content with simply attending weekly worship one to five times per month. The project came about because of my desire for the church to fulfil the commission God placed upon the church. The project was born out of my desire for all members of the congregation to take part in fulfilling the church's commission. Each of the above initial hypotheses was addressed in at least one of the following eight sermons that follow later in this chapter. The sermons served as a tool to invite the people in the pews to join God in God's work by becoming disciples and serving in a ministry compacity.

Qualitative research is the analysis of non-numerical collected data and information to interpret opinions, ideas, or experiences.

The qualitative research tool I used is the mixed-methods case study research approach, in combination with interviews and surveys. From October 2023 to December 2023, I gathered data from multiple people in the congregation who are not actively engaged in the ministry of the church. I interviewed them to discover the reasons as to why they are not actively engaged through a series of open-ended questions. I employed either a structured or semi-structured approach to interviewing to gather the necessary data to complete the project as described in Tim Sensing's *Qualitative Research: A Multi-Methods Approach to Projects for Doctor of Ministry Theses*.

The effectiveness of the sermons was mostly determined by the feedback from the sermon evaluation forms (Appendix B) completed by church members in attendance. The evaluation forms asked the respondents to evaluate the sermon on structure, clarity, relevance, impact, message, and delivery.

Interpretive Perspectives

One of the outcomes of prophetic preaching is to increase interpretive perspectives in terms of the biblical text and the community. It also seeks to engage the biblical text in contemporary critical thought.

Every member of the church has a role to play in God's commission to the church. There is a perception amongst some people in the pews that only certain family members are allowed to serve in any type of ministry capacity. The actions of the church are not always consistent with the words spoken in a sermon. Foley and Anderson say, "One of the critical issues facing congregations of faith is that the practices of a community do not always correspond with what they teach or proclaim themselves to be."[75] When new persons come to the church, the existing members of the church must welcome, engage, and accept them into the congregation while being attentive to how issues they may be going through are addressed. One of the possible reasons church attendance and participation is declining could be because the church insults, judges, mischaracterizes, and demeans the persons it was commanded to make disciples, teach, and baptize.

The sermon titled "A Divine But from Destruction to Deliverance" taken from Genesis 6:17-18. The King James Version (KJV) records, "And, behold, I, even I, do bring a flood of waters upon the earth, to destroy all flesh, wherein is the breath of life, from under heaven; and everything that is in the earth shall die. But with thee will I establish my covenant; and thou shalt come into the ark, thou, and thy sons, and thy wife, and thy sons' wives with thee." Genesis 6:6 records how God felt about the condition and relationship with God's creation. God was sorry and saddened in God's heart how far humanity had fallen into the depths of sin and depravity. The complication in the text is will the righteous be destroyed along with and because of the unrighteous. The resolution

---

[75] Anderson, Herbert and Foley, Edward, *Mighty Stories, Dangerous Rituals: Weaving Together the Human and the Divine,* (San Francisco, CA: Jossey-Bass, A Wiley Company, 1998), 17.

in the text is God's instructions to Noah to build an ark for the deliverance of him and his family. The celebration in the text is because God provided the method of deliverance. Celebration thrives where the glory and goodness of God is evident and undeniable.

Genesis 6:17-18 was chosen as the sermonic text because it was a text most of the listeners would be familiar. The sermon discussed what God included in the building of the ark and also highlighted what God did not include in the building of the ark. That phraseology caught the attention of several listeners. The things God omitted include, doorknobs, oars, and steering, were all items required to control the ark. The sermon caused some of the people in the pews to think about a familiar story with a different lens and more in depth.

Just as Noah had to relinquish control, to have faith in God, and to trust God, the church must relinquish control and follow God's direction to be delivered from the current issue they are facing. The church must recognize that it has all it needs to solve the problem and be the church that God has called it to be. Despite God's disappointment with creation, God did not completely walk away and leave creation to its own vices and choices. The sinfulness of humankind does not negate God's power and ability to restore humankind. God never runs out of options to deliver redemption, salvation, restoration, justification, and regeneration to God's creation. God always possesses the power to make a way out of no way. God's plan for God's creation could not and would not be thwarted by creation's sinfulness.

"A Divine But from Destruction to Deliverance" illustrates to the people in the pews God's power and ability to deliver the righteous and punish the unrighteous simultaneously. The exegetical moves throughout the sermon revealed a new interpretation to some of a familiar scripture passage. One of the exegetical moves revealed the reason for God's decision to destroy God's creation. The sermon highlighted a deeper and more deliberate engagement of the Bible.

"A Divine But from Destruction to Deliverance" is an implicit prophetic sermon. The sermon is a celebratory sermon to encourage the people in the pews to accept God's invitation of deliverance from destruction. The sermon introduced and reminded those in attendance that God provides a method of salvation for God's chosen people.

Celebratory Preaching

Reflecting upon the sermon's text and deeper contemplation upon conversations with the PPG, the moves I made in the sermon intended to address the needs I perceived existing in the congregation. In the sermon I addressed Jesus separating the disciples into two groups, nine disciples in the valley to cast out a demon and three disciples on the mountain to witness the transfiguration. Neither of the two groups of disciples were more important than the other group. Each group had a different role and function in the ministry of Jesus with each role as important as the other.

The celebratory preaching motif tends to end sermons on a more uplifting tone because the Goodness of God always prevails. Good always triumphs over evil. Love always conquers hate. No matter how bad things may seem, everything will work out for the good in the end.

The sermon, "A Glimpse of God's Glory," taken from Matthew 17:1-6 (KJV) reads:

> And after six days Jesus taketh Peter, James, and John his brother, and bringeth them up into an high mountain apart, And was transfigured before them: and his face did shine as the sun, and his raiment was white as the light. And, behold, there appeared unto them Moses and Elias talking with him. Then answered Peter, and said unto Jesus, Lord, it is good for us to be here: if thou wilt, let us make here three tabernacles; one for thee, and one for Moses, and one for Elias. While he yet spake, behold, a bright cloud overshadowed them: and behold a voice out of the cloud, which said, This is my beloved Son, in whom I am well pleased; hear ye him. And when the disciples heard it, they fell on their face, and were sore afraid.

The transfiguration of Jesus on the mountain is a display of God's glory. Peter, James, and John were present to serve as witnesses to this miraculous display. Like the disciples on the mountain, we can also experience a glimpse of God's glory when we are in right relationship with God. On the mountain the glory of God that was enclosed in the body of Jesus was temporarily and partially revealed to the three disciples. The text also says that Moses and Elijah also appeared and had a conversation with Jesus before he was to be tried, convicted, and sentenced to die on the cross. The appearance of Moses represented the law as a reminder to Jesus to remain encouraged to follow God's command completely and not make the same mistake that Moses made. Moses became angry, did not follow God's command completely, and was not allowed to enter the Promised Land. Jesus had to maintain his composure, follow God's command completely, and die on the cross for the salvation of the world. Jesus had to die on the cross for God's creation to become worthy to be in God's presence. The appearance of Elijah represented the prophets as a reminder to Jesus to not become scared and hide from the task he was sent to complete. Elijah encouraged Jesus to not lose courage in the face of danger like he did and get replaced like he did. There is no replacement for Jesus.

Only Jesus, the Only Begotten Son of God, could serve as the mediator between God and God's creation. Only Jesus could die as the propitiation for the sins of the God's creation. Even though Jesus was free from sin and never committed a sin, He took upon Himself all the sins of the world. Through his death, burial and resurrection, God's creation would have the opportunity to be forgiven for their sins and redeemed from their sins.

In the church different people, groups, committees have different roles and functions, but they are all equally important as the others. However, those churches rely heavily upon the most senior members of the congregation to serve in leadership positions. The same people hold most of the decision-making authority. The same people tend to rotate from one ministry position to another. Churches must adopt a more inclusive approach to develop a more functional ministry effort in the church.

The text for this sermon was chosen to engage the people in the pews to encounter God more significantly and intentionally through celebratory preaching per the year's learning goal. The Transfiguration of Jesus Christ is one of many celebratory texts in the Bible. Exegetically the text lends itself to a celebratory conclusion. The glory of God manifested itself on earth in the presence of Jesus Christ. I invited the people in the pews to accept God's revelation of who Jesus is. Today's disciple can witness the goodness, greatness, and manifestation of God.5

"A Glimpse of God's Glory" is a prophetic sermon that addresses a specific issue I observed in the congregation. The congregation was seeking God's guidance on a decision the church was forced to make. The sermon encouraged the factions in the church to remain on one accord, pray without ceasing, and trust God to lead and guide them in the direction God wanted them to go. The sermon also revealed to the church the glorious possibilities that awaits those who trust and depend on God. The sermon also presented to the people in the pews how God reveals Godself to the people in the pews before he or she enters the Kingdom of Heaven.

Integrative Sermon

Many in the church are still talking about the problem instead of working to solve the problem. The church can make a change. However, it may not have the desire to make a change. It may not know how to change or believe there is a need to change. There are too many people who are complaining and criticizing but not willing to work to improve the situation.

The author of I John encourages the early believers of Jesus Christ to remain steadfast and faithful to the word of God as they wait for the return of Jesus Christ. The author in I John 4:14 encourages the recipients of the epistle to follow the apostles' example to testify to what God has done in their life. The sermon invited the people in the pews to testify to what they have seen and heard God do in their individual lives.

The goals of "Can God Get a Witness?" 1) invite people in the congregation to consider God's desire for a deeper, personal, intimate relationship with the people in the pews, and 2) develop and preach sermons to invite people to engage the Bible in a more meaningful way. The sermon highlights how God blesses the believer to be a blessing to others. The sermon encourages hearers to tell God's story based upon what they have seen and heard. The sermon taken from I John 4:13-15 (KJV) which reads, "Hereby know we that we dwell in him, and he in us, because he hath given us of his Spirit. And we have seen and do testify that the Father sent the Son to be the Savior of the world. Whosoever shall confess that Jesus is the Son of God, God dwelleth in him, and he in God." Like John, we, too, must know the Holy Spirit is dwelling within us, speaking to us, speaking through us, and working amongst us. The power of the Holy Spirit is limitless. Through the Holy Spirit, we can do all things God commands us.

"Can God Get a Witness?" identifies six types of witnesses that are present in the Bible to serve as examples that may be present in the church today. There are reluctant witnesses, hostile witnesses, expert witnesses, character witnesses, percipient witnesses, and eyewitnesses. The parents of the man who was born blind and healed by Jesus in John 9:13-27 are one example of a reluctant witness. Peter's denial of being a disciple of Jesus Christ is an example of a hostile witness in Mark 14:66-72. The apostle Paul in Philippians 3:4-8 is an example of an expert witness. The centurion at the cross for the crucifixion of Jesus Christ in Luke 23:47 is an example of a character witness. Mary Magdalene, Peter, and John arriving at the tomb after the resurrection of Jesus in John 20:1-9 are examples of percipient witnesses. John says in I John 4:14 that he was an eyewitness to the miracles, sermons, parables, crucifixion, resurrection, and ascension of Jesus Christ. I had to realize that God just needs me to have faith to stand and God will do the rest. God knows the words that must be spoken and will speak through our voice.

There is a perceived spirit of favoritism and nepotism in the church. There is a sense amongst some in the congregation that their voice is not being heard by the leadership of the church. In Baptist polity, decision-making in the church is done by the people in the pews in agreement with the Word of God as led by the Holy Spirit. There is a perception in the church that not everyone is permitted or encouraged to participate in the ministry and work of the church. The same people rotate through all the leadership and ministry positions in the local congregation. These perceptions must be eliminated for the church to fulfil its role in the spreading the gospel of Jesus Christ. God intentionally desires for every person to function and exercise his or her gift within the mission and ministry of the church.

"Can God Get a Witness?" is another implied prophetic sermon. It was an invitational sermon to invite the people in the pews to become a witnessing servant and to increase their discipleship responsibilities in testifying to the goodness of God. Every believer of Jesus Christ has a witness worth telling. God encourages, expects, and utilizes all types of witnesses to advance the Kingdom of God.

The sermon does not specifically state the problem of the lack of witnesses. It highlights the types of witnesses we can become based upon examples found in the biblical scriptures. The sermon serves as a learning opportunity to engage further sermon development and creativity seeking ways to preach more prophetically in future sermons.

Each person sitting in the pews of the church has been given a vital function to fulfill in the life of the local congregation. God intends for all saved persons to serve God in whatever situations God puts them. Serving God means serving others. Those engaged in the ministry of the church serve on the various committees, boards, and other groups in the church. Those engaged in the ministry of the church seek opportunities to be of service to the church in whatever capacity their gifts, skills and talents lead them.

Interpretative Sermon

Cleophus LaRue suggests the beginning of Black preaching originates from the socioeconomic status of African Americans in this country. LaRue says, "a mighty God who takes up the cause of dispossessed African Americans is the major premise that undergirds the power of black preaching. Those who seek to benefit from this kind of preaching must have an unshakeable faith in this God of the scriptures."[76] African American preachers' interpretation of the biblical scriptures revolve around the thought that God sides with the oppressed, repressed, downtrodden, and abused. God intervenes to improve, rescue, and deliver the oppressed from the negative influences of the oppressor.

"I Am Found" is a sermon that engages the text to remind one of what Kirk Jones says. He writes, "To hear God is to gain a tolerance for my own acceptance, to accept that I am accepted."[77] Listening to God allows the hearer an opportunity to truly commune with God. Listening to God allows the hearer an opportunity to truly be delivered from some past weights and hinderances.

One of the purposes and goals for "I Am Found" was to enhance sermon-crafting and delivery skills to better engage the people in the pews. Another goal was to develop strategies for sparking creativity

---

[76] LaRue, Cleophus J., *"The Heart of Black Preaching"*, (Louisville, KY: Westminster John Knox Press, 2000), 5.
[77] Jones, Kirk Byron, *The Jazz of Preaching: How to Preach with Great Freedom and Joy,* (Nashville, TN: Abingdon Press, 2004), 54.

in the preaching delivery moment. In delivering narrative type sermons, I always seek to identify myself in the narrative. "I Am Found" is a narrative sermon that was delivered is taken from Hosea 1:2; 3:1-3 (KJV). which reads:

> The beginning of the word of the Lord by Hosea. And the Lord said to Hosea, Go, take unto thee a wife of whoredoms and children of whoredoms: for the land hath committed great whoredom, departing from the Lord. Then said the Lord unto me, Go yet, love a woman beloved of her friend, yet an adulteress, according to the love of the Lord toward the children of Israel, who look to other gods, and love flagons of wine. So I bought her to me for fifteen pieces of silver, and for an homer of barley, and an half homer of barley: And I said unto her, Thou shalt abide for me many days; thou shalt not play the harlot, and thou shalt not be for another man: so will I also be for thee.

Everyone who accepts Jesus the Christ as their Lord and personal Savior has a calling upon their lives. The Holy Spirit indwells everyone who accepts Jesus the Christ as their Lord and personal Savior. The Holy Spirit equips every believer with at least one spiritual gift. God intends the believer use the spiritual gift to evangelize the unbeliever, to edify the body of believers, and to prove the power and existence of the Holy Spirit. Pauline theology teaches the believers' salvation exists because of faith in Jesus Christ and not by works. The Holy Spirit puts the believer to work.

"I Am Found" turns into a personal testimony. Because of what

God has done, God's story must be told by every believer. "I Am Found" highlights to the hearer to accept their own duplicitous behaviors, accept God's invitation to be delivered from sin, and join God's team of witnesses. Every believer in Jesus Christ has been found by God. Many believers have returned to the troubles and difficult situations God delivered them from. Everyone has been delivered from something. Discipleship means a calling to tell the story of how God will find you and place you back in right relationship with God.

There have been times in our lives when we have returned to the sinful behavior that God has forgiven and delivered us. On more than one occasion we have repeated of the sinful behavior that we previously promised not to repeat. We have the best intentions to remain committed, faithful, and resolute in my relationship with God but have returned to the sinful behavior God has delivered. The primary point of the sermon was God separates the sin from the sinner. God does not define us by our actions or the sins we commit. There is no place God is not willing to find us. Prayerfully some people in the pews were able to relieve themselves of some burdens God never intends for them to carry.

"I Am Found" is a prophetic sermon in that it presents to the people in the pews the problem that exists in the congregation that it has a problem of returning to the negative behaviors of the past. The sermon highlighted how many people in the pews are hindering their ministry engagement by returning to some old behaviors not conducive to ministry. The sermon then highlights God's efforts to return the believer to right relationship with God. God does recover and redeem.

Monuments and Memorials

"Tell the Story!" is a sermon drawn from Joshua 4:21-24 (KJV) which records:

> And he spake unto the children of Israel, saying, When your children shall ask their fathers in time to come, saying, What mean these stones? Then ye shall let your children know, saying, Israel came over this Jordan on dry land. For the Lord your God dried up the waters of Jordan from before you, until ye were passed over, as the Lord your God did to the Red sea, which he dried up from before us, until we were gone over: That all the people of the earth might know the hand of the Lord, that it is mighty: that ye might fear the Lord your God for ever.

Monuments, memorials, and statues tell a story. They are built and erected so that an event, person, or thing will be forever remembered. Monuments, memorials, and statues are an invitation for visitors to explore, research, and learn more.

"Tell the Story" seeks to help the hearer better understand his or her role in fulfilling the goals and mission of the church. When the believer accepts God's invitation to discipleship, a common set of characteristics are developed in the person's life. A disciple makes a real commitment to be in relationship with Jesus Christ. He or she desires to spend as time as possible learning and studying what it means to serve God. A disciple possesses a spirit of humility to serve whoever, however, and wherever they are directed. A disciple possesses a deep-seated desire to learn. A disciple sees themselves as a perpetual student.

While monuments, memorials, and statues can be a source of memorialization and commemoration, they can also be a source of division, consternation, denial, pain, and selective telling of history. Failure to research the history, meaning, and purpose of any monument can potentially lead to interpretive misunderstandings, misplaced criticisms, and unnecessary hostilities.

Reflecting upon the history, purpose, and effect of Confederate monuments increases reflective thinking of the biblical text for this sermon. God gives Joshua the purpose, history, and eventual effect of the erected stones as recorded in Joshua 4:21-24. God also provides what the purpose and desired result of what all Christian church monuments should be. God tells Joshua to build a monument as a memorial to the miraculous work of God in the life of the children of Israel. God tells Joshua that children will ask their fathers what the meaning of the monument is. The fathers were to take the opportunity to tell the children what God did. Monuments, memorials, and statues in the church should also serve as a reminder to everyone what God has done in the life of the church. Monuments in the church should serve the same purpose and function.

Not only do stones, memorials, and statues tell a story. Every believer of Jesus Christ has a story to tell of how good God is and are a marker to the miraculous, saving power of God through the salvific work of Jesus Christ on the cross. God has done something in the life of every person in the pews. God has performed a miracle in the life of every person in the pews. God desires every person in the pews to tell the story of God and their relationship with God. I am a living, breathing, miracle stone who has a story to tell. The story we tell is less about who we are or what we have done. The story we must tell is more about who God has made us and what God has done in our lives. Lisa Thompson argues the preacher must make a conscious and deliberate decision in what to present and articulate to the church audience. She writes, "It's about determining what matters most and why it matters, and then, proclaiming out of that conviction for the sake of living according to those convictions."[78] When the believer tells the story of a monument, the purpose and focus of the story is always to highlight the grace, mercy, and goodness of God. Deciding what to include and exclude should always be guided by what illustrates the glory of God the most. In telling the believers' story, God's story will ultimately be told.

"Tell the Story!" was a prophetic sermon that built upon "I Am Found." It encouraged the people in the pews to take the next step once they have been found. God invites the people in the pews to tell what God has done in their life. Blessings can be found in telling the story. Our stories become part of God's story of God's relationship with God's creation.

---

[78] Thompson, Lisa, Preaching the Headlines: Possibilities and Pitfalls, (Minneapolis, MN: Fortress Press, 2021), 117.

Integrative Sermon

The sermon titled "Trouble Don't Last Always" develops from I Peter 5:8-10 (KJV) which records:

> Be sober, be vigilant; because your adversary the devil, as a roaring lion, walketh about, seeking whom he may devour: same afflictions are accomplished in your brethren that are in the world. But the God of all grace, who hath called us unto his eternal glory by Christ Jesus, after that ye have suffered a while, make you perfect, stablish, strengthen, settle you.

Peter uses one characteristic of a lion to encourage and remind the believer to be alert and aware of the devil's presence. Peter tells the church to be alert, vigilant, and always mindful of the devil. Peter says the devil is like a lion on the prowl. Lions do not roar very often. Lions roar to frighten away other animals. Lions roar in anger when fighting.

The lion characteristic that Peter compared to the devil involves the animal's hunting methods. Lions are predatory stalkers. Lions can be extremely silent when approaching an animal for prey. Because of the colors of their fur, lions can easily camouflage themselves in the jungle's foliage. When stalking their prey, lions excel in identifying the weaknesses of their prey. Lions always attack their prey from behind. The lion kills its prey by biting its throat and crushing its windpipe. Peter cautioned the believer to always be on alert for the presence of the devil. Like the lion, the devil is a predatory stalker. The devil excels are looking for weaknesses in the life of the believer. Like the lion, the devil does a masterful job at disguising himself in the surroundings of the believer. Like the lion, the devil pounces, and attacks when the believer is at their weakest and most vulnerable. Like the lion, the devil attempts to kill the believer's relationship with God by crushing the believer's faith, hope, belief, and trust in God.

Our relationship with God is based around our faith and belief that Jesus Christ is the only Begotten Son of God. We are saved by our confessed faith. The Holy Spirit then indwells us individually, gifts us purposefully, and then directs us to complete a work. Our relationship with God does not exempt us from experiencing times of hardship and trouble. In times of trouble, all of us need to be reminded that trouble does not always last. The II Peter sermonic text is chosen as an encouragement to remain committed, to stay vigilant, and to never give up. The biblical text concludes with a prayer to God from Peter. He knows the suffering and dangers Christians may face. He asks God to make perfect, to establish, and to strengthen the believer. God works these things into and through the life of the believer. Peter serves as an example to the Christian believer.

Post sermon contemplations and meditations of the sermon reveals a move that could have been made in the sermon but omitted. A good sermonic move would have been to include how God handled times of trouble. Even though God will never leave us during our times of trouble, God experienced times of trouble. Genesis 6:6 says God was grieved in his heart because of the actions of the greatest in Creation. Those were troubling times for God. The children of Israel caused God to experience times of heartbreak and distress while they were wondering through the wilderness to the Promised Land. God experienced additional periods of trouble when the children of Israel were living in the Promised Land. The passing of Lazarus in the eleventh chapter of John was a troubling time for Jesus. He was heartbroken when he experienced and saw the sadness and mourning of Mary and Martha. Jesus wept himself and was troubled in his spirit. While praying in the Garden of Gethsemane in Matthew 26, Jesus became sorrowful and troubled in his spirit. In Matthew's crucifixion narrative, Jesus experiences troubling times before his death. Not only does Jesus experience pain because of his physical torment, he experiences spiritual trouble and torment because his relationship with God changed. Jesus feels forsaken by God. Jesus feels separated from God. Jesus feels betrayed because of God. For one brief moment, the relationship is not a Father-Son relationship. For one moment, the relationship is a God-sin relationship. The forsakenness Jesus felt caused him to ask God, why.

"Trouble Don't Last Always" was a prophetic sermon in that it presented the need to make disciples. It also highlighted what discipleship creates in the body of believers. The sermon presented the challenges and hindrances to the disciple-making process the people in the pews should be aware of and fight against. The adversary put obstacles and roadblocks in the path of obedience to God's Word. The sermon presented to the people in the pews the ultimate defeat of the adversary and what the image of success will look like.

Ministry Assessment Survey

A survey of the church members who regularly attend weekly worship services to gain more insight into why most of the people in the pews are not engaged in the ministry of the church is conducted. The survey attempts to reach a large enough number of respondents to be able to properly analyze the feedback received. The survey response rate was twenty-two percent. According to a quick online search, the average survey response rate is sixteen to thirty-three percent.[79]

The survey sought input from the church members on their current level of understanding of the ministry of the church. The survey also asked members if they know what their spiritual gift is and to identify the gift. The interviews explored why some members of the church seem to want to maintain a connection with the church but are not working within the church.

---

[79] The following sites reported this range: Chung, Lucia, *"What is a good survey response rate for online customer surveys?,"* https://delighted.com/blog/average-survey-response-rate#:~:text=These%20response%20rate%20benchmarks%20are%20usually%20qualified%20by,survey%20response%20rate%20for%20NPS%20surveys%20%28Genroe%2C%202019%29, assessed on December 11, 2023, and Vianna, Carla, *"Survey Benchmarks: What's a good survey response rate?,"* https://www.xola.com/articles/survey-benchmarks-whats-a-good-survey-response-rate/, assessed on December 11, 2023, and Customer Thermometer, "Average Survey Response Rate - What You Need to Know," https://www.customerthermometer.com/customer-surveys/average-survey-response-rate/, assessed on December 11, 2023.

Social Transformation Sermon

The purpose and goal of the sermon was to expand the congregation's thinking of social transformation and present how the role of preaching fits within the context of the church's ministry. The sermon enlightened and enlivened my personal thinking of what the church can accomplish. Social transformation forces the preacher to envision a brighter future and to not accept the status quo.

The sermon titled "Jesus Paid It All" is taken from Romans 6:23 (KJV) and reads, "For the wages of sin is death; but the gift of God is eternal life through Jesus Christ our Lord." The sermonic issue addressed in the sermon is community crime and violence. It investigates the issue by examining and analyzing crime data in the neighborhood surrounding the church. According to the Minnesota State Crime Database, a crime is committed in the area around the church every three hours and forty-nine minutes. The types of crime committed at that rate are either personal against an individual or property. The types of personal crimes committed are assault, battery, homicide, manslaughter, kidnapping, abuse, and rape. The types of property crimes committed are burglary, robbery, vandalism, arson, shoplifting, and trespassing.

One disturbing and revealing factor is that race and income are defining characteristics in state and local criminal justice systems. People of color are dramatically over-represented in Minnesota prisons and jails. African Americans are incarcerated at a much higher rate than any other race.[80] In St. Paul forty-five percent of male incarcerations are African American, and twenty nine percent are African American for female incarcerations, while the city population of African Americans is about two percent. Poverty is also a conditional factor of crime, violence, and incarceration.

To reduce the level of crime and violence in the community, the church must have a multi-pronged approach to alleviate the problem. The church must partner with other churches, civic organizations, public and private schools, charities, businesses, and corporations. No one group can solve the problem alone. All interested parties must come together and have what Gregory Ellison II calls a "fearless dialogue."[81] Ellison believes social transformation can be achieved when opposing stakeholders enter the same space to engage in difficult, challenging, and painful conversations working to achieve a common goal. Ellison believes change happens best when entities understand and see each other's viewpoints. He writes, "Hard heartfelt conversation with unlikely partners rarely unfolds unless the company of strangers are welcomed with Radical Hospitality and made to feel at home."[82] Social transformation can be achieved when unlikely partners sit together in the same space to discuss diverse ways of dealing with conflict. Societies and communities can be socially transformed by

---

[80] Wagner P, Sawyer W. Mass incarceration: the whole pie 2018. Prison Policy Initiative. 2018. https://www.prisonpolicy.org/ reports/pie2018.html. Published March 14, 2018. Accessed September 8, 2023.
[81] Ellison II, Greggory, *Fear+less Dialogues: A New Movement for Justice*, (Nashville, TN: Westminster John Knox Press, 2017), 6.
[82] Ibid., 33.

encouraging community partners who seemingly have nothing in common to come together and find common ground.

The sermon presents a new vision of what the surrounding community and the future community could and should be. The sermon's vision of a new community is one that is free from fear. With the power of the Holy Spirit undergirding the church, a community can be created where the elderly can live in tents under a fig tree with no fear as prophesied in Micah chapter four. The power of the Holy Spirit can lead the church to create a community where children can play in the streets without fear as prophesied in Zechariah chapter eight. The church has the power to facilitate social transformation where everyone can achieve the highest education level they desire.

The church has the power to facilitate social transformation where the unemployment rate is near zero and everyone earns wages to allow them to live comfortably with all their needs met. The church has the power to facilitate social transformation where race and gender are not impediments to wealth, employment, and education. Gregory Ellison II writes, "the human capacity to imagine enables us to form mental pictures of our self, our neighbor, our world, and our future. This ability to envision new realities engages and transforms."[83] Under the unction of the Holy Spirit, the church can envision a new world order where God is glorified and the peace on earth outlined in the Bible is created. The church

---

[83] Ellison, *Fear+less Dialogues: A New Movement for Justice*, 25.

envisions a community where swords are beaten into plowshares, lions lay down with the lambs, and the children play in the snake's den. More importantly, the sermon closes with a vision of the community and the church God ordains based upon the Word of God.

Community Justice Sermon

Preaching can be used to highlight how others may have a different viewpoint on justice. Some preaching strategies can maximize the congregation's willingness to engage and minimize the possibility of resistance. Oftentimes justice is in the eye of the beholder. A person's ideologies, context, history, and socioeconomics are all variables in his or her idea of justice. The sermon "Tell Egypt Goodbye" draws from Exodus 14:11-14 (KJV) which reads:

And they said unto Moses, Because there were no graves in Egypt, hast thou taken us away to die in the wilderness? wherefore hast thou dealt thus with us, to carry us forth out of Egypt? Is not this the word that we did tell thee in Egypt, saying, Let us alone, that we may serve the Egyptians? For it had been better for us to serve the Egyptians, than that we should die in the wilderness. And Moses said unto the people, Fear ye not, stand still, and see the salvation of the Lord, which he will shew to you to day: for the Egyptians whom ye have seen to day, ye shall see them again no more for ever. The Lord shall fight for you, and ye shall hold your peace.

The focus of the sermon is to deliver a message from a biblical text that addresses the topic of transformational justice. The sermon addresses the lack of ministry participation and membership absenteeism amongst the people in the pews. Church ministry requires an all-hands-on-deck strategy.

When God reveals to the preacher an issue in the church, the community, and the life of the believer, the preacher is compelled and directed to address the issue as directed by the Holy Spirit. Local congregations cannot continue to exist as they always have. Otherwise, the decline in attendance, ministry engagement and biblical literacy will continue its negative, downward trend.[84] The preacher is compelled to allow the Holy Spirit to sermonically invite the people in the pews to become what God has called and ordained them. O. Wesley Allen says, "it's important to remember that it is not the preacher's job simply to preach the gospel; it is the preacher's job to get the gospel heard, then believed, and then lived."[85] There are many persons in the church with many skills, abilities, and talents. The differences in gifts, skills, abilities, and functions do not elevate one member over another. All are important to the ministry and function of the church. In completing its ministry, the church must remain steadfast in allowing God to show them the direction God chooses to lead them. God is still telling the disciples in the church that Jesus is God's Beloved, Well-Pleasing

[84] Lugo, Luis and Stencel, Sandra, *U.S. Religious Landscape Survey, Religious Beliefs and Practices: Diverse and Politically Relevant*, (Washington, D.C.: Pew Forum Web Publishing, 2008), 36.

[85] Allen, Jr., O. Wesley, *Preaching in the Era of Trump*, (Nashville, TN: Chalice Press, 2017), 20.

Son and that the church must listen to him.

The sermonic presentation of "Tell Egypt Goodbye" presents to the people in the pews how the Holy Spirit embodies each of them with a spiritual gift and that God intends for them to use that spiritual gift to evangelize the lost and to edify the body of Jesus Christ. The sermon highlights how everyone is needed and required to serve in the ministry of the church. The current rate of participation in some churches does not provide long term ministry stability or success.

"Tell Egypt Goodbye" was a prophetic sermon that encouraged the people in the pews to leave negative, painful experiences in the past. The sermon presented the existing problem of continuing to hold on to some of the negative events in its history. Those issues are hindering the advancement of the church in some areas and are a turnoff to some of the potential new members. The sermon also presented a great vision of what community will look like when the people in the pews leave the negative past in the past and march into a bright future.

Sermon Analysis Conclusions

Earlier in the book, the level of church ministry engagement was stated to be about twenty to thirty percent based upon observational data. Active ministry engagement is defined as serving on at least one committee, board, choir, or auxiliary and a regular attendee of Sunday School or Bible Study. Serving in some ministry allows believers to exercise the spiritual gift every believer has been endowed with by the Holy Spirit. Attending Bible Study or Sunday

School allows believers to increase their biblical literacy and knowledge of the Word of God. Not only does Bible Study and Sunday School increase biblical literacy, but they also build church community and relationships in the church.

Some ministry leaders of the church are receptive to the assessment that the level of church ministry engagement as unacceptable and unsustainable. The ministry leaders of the church welcomed and are looking forward to recommendations on how to increase the ministry engagement of the people in the pews.

A church wide survey to gauge the ministry interests of the people in the pews should be conducted to determine if there is a gap between where the people's interest lies and the existing ministries of the church. Typically, the church offers the same traditional groups and ministries that have been in existence for decades. Ministry groups may need to be updated or created to meet the needs of the people in the pews.

Chapter Six

Results and Evaluation

The integrative sermon, Trouble Don't Last Always," talked about in the previous chapter, was critiqued by some of the persons in attendance. The sermon evaluation form asked for a rating of the sermon on a scale of zero to five (highest). The first question was: did the title of the sermon accurately reflect the content of the sermon? The average of all respondents was five point zero. The second question: was the content of the sermon anchored in the sermonic text? The average of all respondents was five point zero. The third question was: how clear was the objective of the sermon? The average of all respondents was four point eight two. One hundred percent of the respondents said the audience was the right audience for this message.

Question number seven of the survey asked the respondents: "What did you learn from the sermon and how has it impacted your life?" Below are some of the responses that were submitted:

1. Both the sermon and the scripture text give me hope that when things are not going right, that things will only be

difficult for a while – in other words "Trouble Don't Last Always!"[86]

2. Suffering is a part of my Christian journey; it's going to happen; I must keep the faith. Restoration is promised.[87]

3. Saints will suffer; however, the suffering is only for a while.[88]

4. I learned that in life trials and tribulations may come but through faith GOD can strengthen us and settle us.[89]

5. The sermon gave me a new perspective on life. I gained strength and assurance in being reminded that I have riches and blessings stored up for me that are greater than I can ever imagine.[90]

6. It contained direct encouragement and hope that sounded from the preacher's personal experience and connected well to the text. The use of Peter and his discipling experience was particularly well done. We can all relate to Peter's character flaws.[91]

The sermon seems to have been well received by the people in the pews. The problem has been identified from the pulpit and presented to the people in the pews. Cedric E.W. Vine says, "Prophets

---

[86] Althea Rupert, PPG Sermon Feeback Form, November 28, 2022.

[87] Clarence Kenon, PPG Sermon Feeback Form, November 28, 2022.

[88] Sheila James, PPG Sermon Feeback Form, November 28, 2022.

[89] John James, PPG Sermon Feeback Form, November 28, 2022.

[90] Arlander Gathing, PPG Sermon Feeback Form, November 28, 2022

[91] Albert Goins, PPG Sermon Feeback Form, November 28, 2022.

diagnose the problem and warn the nation of the consequences."[92] Change has been difficult to institute.

Humor, personal struggles, shortcomings, and failings have been tools that were utilized to present the message of the sermon completely, honestly, and openly. For the message to be received by the people in the pews, the preacher must connect with the people in the pews. The people in the pews must feel as if the preacher is speaking directly to them, addressing each of their specific needs, and is personally engaging in the struggles they are enduring. Karen Wiseman says:

> Sitting in the pews on a typical Sunday, the people who come to our worship services want to hear a Word from the Lord that challenges them, that inspires them, that educates them, that engages their senses and passions, that encourages them to live more faithfully, that prepares them for the coming week, that lifts their spirits, that brings the Word into their own experiences, and that makes a difference in the way they approach their own struggles and life experiences.[93]

The sermons should not solely be about the person delivering the message. He or she are messengers. Jesus Christ is the subject. Jesus Christ is the message. Jesus Christ is the gospel.

The Bible is a living, breathing organism. The lessons and messages are still applicable today. The lessons, messages, and

---

[92] Vine, Cedric E.W., *Jesus and the Nations: Discipleship and Mission in the Gospel of Matthew*, (Eugene, OR: Pickwick Publications, 2022), 165.
[93] Wiseman, Karen L. I Refuse to Preach a Boring Sermon! Engaging the 21st Century Listener, (Cleveland, OH: Pilgrim Press, 2013), 13-14.

words did not die when the earthly writers died. The preacher should bring as much life to the words of the Bible as possible. The biblical writers used a myriad of literary tools to illustrate the words they received from God. They used words to paint a visual picture for the hearers and readers of God's word. Consequently, the preacher should be mindful of word choice in presenting the sermon to the people in the pews. I was reminded of Wiseman's words, "for preaching to ignite the fires in the belly of those hearing the sermon there needs to be something to catch their imagination, to spark their creative thoughts, and to push their minds to see where the word, sermon, and the preacher are going."[94] In order to catch the imagination of the people in the pews, I relate to them where I identify the most in the biblical text.

Deliverance Sermon

The sermon, "Tell Egypt Goodbye," talked about in the previous chapter, was critiqued by some of the persons in attendance. The sermon evaluation form asked for a rating of the sermon on a scale of zero to five (highest). The first question was: did the title of the sermon accurately reflect the content of the sermon? The average of all respondents was five point zero. The second question: was the content of the sermon anchored in the sermonic text? The average of all respondents was five point zero. The third question was: how clear was the objective of the sermon? The average of all

---

[94] Wiseman, Karen L. I Refuse to Preach a Boring Sermon! Engaging the 21st Century Listener, 47.

respondents was four point eight six.

Question number seven of the survey asked the respondents: "What did you learn from the sermon and how has it impacted your life?" Below are some of the responses that were submitted:

1. When God makes a way for us, we need to fully embrace what He is doing in our lives and not look back. We also need to recognize that it was God who made a way out of no way.[95]

2. 3 out of 10 does all the work (not effective evangelism)[96]

3. We must trust and believe that God is Able to carry you through any hardships or obstacles you may be enduring at any given time. If He brings you to it, He will carry you through it. The sermon simply just reminded me to continue to trust and believe in God no matter what the world may throw at you.[97]

4. We all have a job to do, and we should be making disciples as we spread the good news of the gospel. Go![98]

5. That we must have faith to "be still" and await the Lord's guidance and solution to our most overwhelming problems and challenges. The subtext or secondary message was that we can know this by reflecting on the seemingly insurmountable problems which God has defeated in the

---

[95] Althea Rupert, PPG Sermon Feeback Form, November 27, 2023
[96] Danny Gladney, PPG Sermon Feeback Form, November 27, 2023.
[97] Sheila James, PPG Sermon Feeback Form, November 27, 2023.
[98] John James, PPG Sermon Feeback Form, November 27, 2023

past. Now we must have the faith to realize he will do that in the present and in the future.[99]

6. We have been falling short on our job. Everyone needs to show up for duty (30 % or 3 out of 10 people are doing the work of the church.) We have become comfortable sitting inside the 4 walls of the church. We romanticize chaos, disfunction, craziness. We speak of how great it used to be when we are asked to make a change.[100]

There seems to be an interest and a desire by some to increase their ministry engagement level. The church needs to hear the message from more than one preacher. Some members in the congregation agree and recognize there is a need to make a change and do something to address the decline in church ministry engagement.

The sermon was almost a sermon within a sermon. It took the opportunity to speak clearly and directly to the issue of having only thirty percent of church members involved in the ministry of the church. There was not a strong connection between the sermonic text and the non-involved seventy percent. The latter portion of the sermon provided the exegesis of the sermonic text.

"Tell Egypt Goodbye," taken from Exodus 14:11-14, and "A Divine But from Destruction to Deliverance," taken from Genesis 6:17-18 deliver similar messages. Their messages are that God makes provisions for the declared righteous to be delivered from destruction. The method of deliverance God provides may be

---

[99] Albert Goins, PPG Sermon Feeback Form, November 27, 2023.
[100] Clarence Kenon, PPG Sermon Feeback Form, November 27, 2023.

unconventional, unusual, and unorthodox, but the true believer must adhere to them completely, explicitly, and faithfully. The sermons reveal the current state of ministry engagement is not hopeless. The situation can be reversed. The situation must be reversed. The situation will be reversed.

Ministry Goals / Path Forward

Observational and collected data suggests: 1) some of the people in the pews are not aware of the existing ministry efforts in the church; 2) overall the people in the pews are interested in increasing their current level of ministry involvement; 3) the ministry leadership must make a direct, personal appeal to the people in the pews; 4) the church cannot rely too heavily on electronic technology to communicate to the people in the pews; 5) there is a disconnect between church leadership and laity on how to best increase church membership.

Based on the collected data, full implementation requires further effort and a deliberate determination to see the expected outcomes to come to fruition. Some of the people in the pews express a desire to be involved in the ministry of the church. The sermons effectively highlighted the need for all people to become involved and participate in the ministry of the church. The data also suggests the explanation of discipleship during the sermons was understood and believed by the people in the pews.

The first goal addressed was the primary concern of the church is to make disciples. The sermon, "Jesus Paid It All," presented most directly and succinctly God's call of discipleship to the people in the pews. The sentiment of some ministry leaders is that the message is applicable and needs to be reiterated for everyone to get on board.

The second goal addressed was to define discipleship in the life of the everyday believer. The sermon, "Tell Egypt Goodbye," defined most directly and succinctly what discipleship looks like in the life of the believer. The sermon defined a disciple as a student, pupil, or learner. The sermon also highlighted that disciples of Jesus Christ make God their focus and make serving God a central priority. Disciples serve God by serving others. Disciples do not define their personal successes by the terms of society or cultural groups. Disciples realize all he or she has or has achieved is through the grace and mercy of God. The sermon also highlighted the call to discipleship is also a call to serve in a ministry in the church.

The third goal the sermons addressed was to invite the people in the pews to increase their ministry engagement in the church. The sermon, "Tell the Story!," instructed the people in the pews that they were invited, asked, and encouraged to participate in the ministry of the church. Everyone has a gift to perform a function in the ministry of the church. The sermon informed that God invites, equips, and expects every believer to perform their function in the church's ministry.

Conclusions

Identifying ministry needs and desires from the people in the pews is not an easy task. Implementation of those identified ministries is even more challenging. Lack of knowledge and awareness of existing ministry activities seem to have been revealed as an issue. The church must initiate a direct appeal outreach strategy to all members on the active roster. The church must move beyond just communicating on its website or strolling announcements. The ministry's appeal for members should become more of a personal appeal. Additionally, the direct appeal to its members would grant ministry leadership the opportunity to gauge what ministry activities the people in the pews are looking to participate in.

There is a desperate need for prophetic preaching that can encourage and inspire the people in the pews to use their spiritual gifts to serve God by serving God's people. Embodied discipleship begins in the local congregation and then extends outside the walls of the church to recapture the essence of Jesus' earthly ministry that meets the needs of people in the church and surrounding communities.

Impact on the Preacher

There is great potential amongst the people in the pews. The church has a plethora of resources at its disposal. The church is not fully utilizing those resources. Prophetic preaching must still speak to the issues and deficiencies of what is, it must also avoid turning off the people it is seeking to encourage and invite. Prophetic preaching is a vital component that must be kept in front of the people.

Impact on Preaching

Modern day preaching should not engage in topic avoidance. Effective preaching encourages and invites the people in the pews to engage in issues that impact the community on a personal and societal level. Biblically and historically, the church through prophetic preaching has been the voice of the community to address issues of social injustice, systemic racism, systemic discrimination, wealth inequality, elder care and abuse, education reform, prison reform, health care disparity, and mental health advocacy. Effective preaching can present the ideal model for interpersonal relationships.

This thesis further contends that each member must understand, know, and rely upon their spiritual gift to successfully fulfil his or her role in the ministry of the church. God gives spiritual gifts for the purpose of building up the church, locally and universally.

The unique outcome of this thesis that impacts preaching is the discipleship component of prophetic preaching that moves from the personal to the communal. The church cannot operate as it always has and allow the decline in ministry engagement to continue. This project argued that prophetic preaching can identify the problem, offer solutions, and provide a plan to implement the solution.

Impact on the Congregation

The primary impact of this project upon the local congregation is to remind them of their capabilities. The church is still able to turn things around and reverse the negative trend that is currently happening within the congregation. The sermons for this project were aimed at reminding the church of their God-given command and responsibility. They were intended to lead the body of believers to realize a change had to be made. The collective messages of the sermons were similar to what is recorded in II Kings 7:3 (KJV), "And there were four leprous men at the entering in of the gate: and they said one to another, Why sit we here until we die?" The church was shown through the series of sermons that things would not automatically change. Waiting for a change without any action from the people in the pews was no longer an option. Prophetic preaching stated with conviction that Pilgrim would not sit and wait to die.

Chapter Seven

Homiletical Significance

The challenge may be daunting; however, it is not insurmountable. God is on the side of the church. The church must stay on God's side. Through the power of the Holy Spirit, God can perform a mighty, miraculous work in the life of the church. Prophetic preaching is a change agent to bring about the church's necessary transformation. Walter Brueggeman says, "Prophetic proclamation is an attempt to imagine the world as though YHWH-the creator of the world, the deliverer of Israel, the Father of our Lord Jesus Christ whom we Christians come to name as Father, Son and Spirit - were a real character and an effective agent in the world."[101] The church must never believe the problem is too large to be overcome. God has already provided The church with all resources necessary to solve the problem. The Holy Spirit is available to lead and guide the people to remedy the solution.

The relationship between the Holy Trinity serves as the model by

---

[101] Brueggemann, Walter, *The Practice of Prophetic Imagination: Preaching an Emancipating Word,* (Minneapolis: Fortress Press, 2012), 3.

which the members of the church must interact with each other. For the whole body to fully function, each member of the body must fulfil his or her role. It is inspiring and encouraging to be a part of the church's potential to fulfil its God-given command.

The sermons were able to present to the people in the pews of God's desire for them to join God in God's work of spreading the gospel of Jesus Christ. The sermons also presented a vision of the church's giftedness through the presence of the Holy Spirit. Brueggeman says, "prophetic preaching is the enactment of hope in contexts of loss and grief."[102] Preaching showcases the existing state of the church's condition and presents a vision of what is possible. Brueggeman writes, prophetic preaching "begins in wonder concerning the inexplicable abundance willed by God the creator."[103] The sermonic presentations afford the opportunity to step into the role of a prophet to declare the word of God and to present God's vision of what God desires for the church. Brueggeman says, prophetic preaching "attests to the power of YHWH to create new historical possibilities where there is no ground for expectation."[104] The future of the church is bright. God will awaken a spiritual revival within the people in the pews that allows them to live up to their calling.

---

[102] Brueggemann, *The Practice of Prophetic Imagination: Preaching an Emancipating Word*, 110.
[103] Ibid., 11.
[104] Ibid., 11.

Impact on the People in the Pews

Institutional change is not easy. If it was easy, everyone would be doing it. Many churches are in a state of declining and aging membership, reduction in financial contributions, and an aging church building. COVID-19 has had an overall negative impact on the ministry activities that the church still has not recovered. Additionally, the church is attempting to navigate its current congregational state against the background of a rich, impactful history. It is grappling with how to engage a population most effectively with many other competing personal interests.

Impact on the Ministry Context

The church has great resources, gifts, skills, talents, and abilities. It has been used by God to be a voice of moral clarity and change in local, state, and national issues. It fought for institutional change by building a coalition of churches, civic organizations, and community groups. It maintains and nurtures its ecumenical relationships with other churches and denominations. Simply put, the decline in church membership has caused a decline in external, outside-the-four-walls activities.

The primary impact of this project upon the church is to remind it of their capabilities. The church is still able to turn things around and reverse the negative trend that is currently happening within the congregation. The sermons were aimed at reminding the church of their God-given command and responsibility. They were intended to lead the body of believers to realize a change had to be made. The collective messages of the sermons were similar to what is recorded in II Kings 7:3 (KJV), "And there were four leprous men at the entering in of the gate: and they said one to another, Why sit we here until we die?" The church is shown through the series of sermons that things will not automatically change. Waiting for a change without any action from the people in the pews was no longer an option. Prophetic preaching stated with conviction that the church cannot sit and wait to die.

Impact on the Field of Homiletics

Prophetic preaching is a homiletical tool that can be used to address a myriad of issues, problems, and difficulties. There is significant amount of scholarship on biblical interpretation, exegesis, and exaltation in preaching. Prophetic preaching is an area of theological study that may not have received as much attention, research, and exploration as it had a few years ago. Modern prophetic preaching must follow the model of biblical prophets. They understood God gave them a call to speak to the people on issues displeasing to God and having an adverse effect on God's people. The biblical prophets were so convinced of God's calling upon their lives that they were willing to risk their livelihood, lifestyle, freedom, and life to speak out against injustice. Modern day preaching must feel the same calling from God upon their lives to speak out against today's societal issues.

This thesis contends that the church cannot continue to function as it has been for the past thirty to forty years. The church cannot complete its commission commanded from Jesus Christ without all members of the church fulfilling their role. The thesis presents the role of prophetic preaching to state the current declining activity of the church, the importance of discipleship in the lives of the people in the pews, and the necessity of a synergetic relationship amongst all church members.

The thesis addresses the importance for the church to exist. God created the church as God's vehicle in which the salvific work on the cross is to spread throughout the entire word. The witness of God by the church is not optional. It is a necessity. The thesis also highlights to the church that God's will and purpose for the church does not change.

The thesis adds to the field of homiletics the importance of prophetic preaching to address the social injustices plaguing the world. Today's Prophetic preaching should follow the model of the biblical prophets. The biblical prophets were led by God to address all social injustices, religious malpractices, and personal shortcomings directly and succinctly. They also presented God's vision of the ideal society in which God's people were to live. Prophetic preaching has been shown God's vision of the ideal modern-day society in which God's people are to live.

The largest contribution to homiletics this thesis presents is the importance of true discipleship for the people in the pews. Discipleship is the relationship model between God and the people in the pews. Discipleship is a lifelong commitment for the new convert to be in relationship with God and fulfil the command God gives to the convert. True discipleship is also formed amongst a group of believers in the community. True discipleship then develops and grows to teaching others the ways in which to follow God for themselves.

Prayerfully, this thesis will be studied, critiqued, and implemented in more contexts to advance homiletical scholarship. Many churches are struggling to increase the level of ministry engagement amongst the people in the pews. Prophetic preaching as presented in this thesis may serve as a bridge between the preacher in the pulpit and the people in the pews.

Final Thoughts / Conclusion

The church must guard itself from becoming a lukewarm church like the Laodicean church in the third chapter of Revelations. Lukewarm churches are neither hot nor cold. Lukewarm churches run the risk of becoming irrelevant because they may be vibrant in some areas but equally stagnant in other areas. For example, they may be vibrant and active in speaking out against issues of social injustice, crime, and discrimination but stagnant in presenting the salvific work of Jesus Christ on the cross.

Some of the reasons people in the pews are not actively involved in the ministry of the local congregation are: 1) no one has ever asked them to; 2) they believe that someone else will do it or the church has a preferred list of people to serve; 3) they feel that the church wants everyone to do things the way they always have and are not open to new thoughts or ideas; 4) some people in the pews do not take the time to learn the polity, practices, history, vision, and mission of the church; 5) Pilgrim is an amalgamation of multiple denominational beliefs, polities, ideologies, and practices.

The ways in which the church can better engage the people to become more involved in the ministry of the church: 1) ask them directly with a personal one on one appeal; 2) teach a spiritual gifts class to define spiritual gifts and their importance, and to help the people potentially identify their individual spiritual gifts; 3) expand Shepherding Ministry to focus on current members as well as onboarding new members; 4) re-establish the Evangelism Ministry; 5) create opportunities to include always include members who are not participating in ministry activities and leadership opportunities.

Chapter Eight

Summary Reflections and Conclusions

Seventy percent of church membership is not involved in the ministry of the church because they do not feel they have a role to play in the ministry the church. Some of them fell that the church has functioned without them in the past and can continue to function without them in the future. Some also believe the church is cliquish and they will not be accepted or received by the perceived powers that be. Secondly, some also do not what their spiritual gift is and do not understand how their spiritual gift fits within the ministry of the church. Thirdly, some of church membership do not understand what the first primary concern of the church is. Finally, seventy percent do not see ministry engagement as being a central component of their lives. They are content with simply attending weekly worship one to five times per month. The project came about because of my desire for the church to fulfil the commission God placed upon the church. The project was born out of the desire for all members of the congregation to take part in fulfilling the church's commission.

Some of the additional reasons for the lack of ministry engagement are the lack of inclusion of new members by the more senior members of the congregation. Church leadership tends to continually rely upon and utilize the same members. Some new congregants do not take time to learn the polity structure and the way the church functions and operates. Existing church members are not always receptive to the new and fresh perspective new members bring to the local congregation.

The reversal of the disturbing and challenging trend that is common in many of today's Christian churches is not impossible. The church must adopt a deliberate and intentional change strategy to see meaningful change.

The first step of a strategy to increase level of ministry engagement in the church is to conduct a spiritual gifts exploration and assessment class for all people in the pews. The identification of each person's spiritual gift or gifts will allow that person to serve in the best ministry capacity of the church. The next step of the process is to make a deliberate effort to ask each person to serve in a ministry capacity if they do not voluntarily come forward on their own initiative. The next step involves creating a spiritual mentoring program to partner with new members of the church. The spiritual mentor will be tasked with teaching the new member church polity, doctrine, history, and structure of the church. The spiritual mentor will also be tasked with bringing ideas, suggestions, and thoughts from the new member to the church leadership team.

My brother and I lived with our grandparents for six years. My grandfather was a positive role model and taught me the value of hard work. He was one of the hardest working men I have ever known. As I am writing, I have a picture in my mind of him walking behind a plow pulled by two mules. He provided for all seventeen of his children and several grandchildren with those seventeen mules. My grandparents' house was small. It was filled with laughter, food, and an abundance of love. Their house was a sanctuary and, seemingly, all were welcome.

My grandfather also believed in education. When I graduated from high school and left for college, he told me to "make sure I get something in my head. If you put something in your head, no one can ever take it away from you." In simple words, he taught me to study hard, learn my chosen field of study, and graduate with more than just a piece of paper. I am proud to be my grandfather's grandson. With a limited education who was discriminated against in rural Mississippi, he provided me with food, shelter, and modeled for me Christian discipleship. Because of his hard work, I have earned a bachelor's degree, a master's degree, and a candidate for a doctorate degree. My grandfather's mules did not ride in the wagon, and they did their job.

As I am writing, I have a picture in my mind of him walking behind a plow pulled by two mules. He provided for all seventeen of his children and several grandchildren with those seventeen mules. My grandparents' house was small. It was filled with laughter, food, and an abundance of love. Their house was a sanctuary and, seemingly, all were welcome.

My grandfather also believed in education. When I graduated from high school and left for college, he told me to "make sure I get something in my head. If you put something in your head, no one can ever take it away from you." In simple words, he taught me to study hard, learn my chosen field of study, and graduate with more than just a piece of paper. I am proud to be my grandfather's grandson. With a limited education who was discriminated against in rural Mississippi, he provided me with food, shelter, and modeled for me Christian discipleship. Because of his hard work, I have earned a Bachelor's degree, a Master's degree, and a Doctor of Ministry degree.

My grandfather's mules never rode in the wagon. They were instrumental and played an active role in the life and survival of our family that continues to thrive and achieve to this day. With those mules and a limited education, my grandfather provided for his descendants who served in the Korean and Vietnam Wars, enlisted in all branches of the military, graduated from high school and college with bachelor's, master's, and doctorate degrees. His descendants serve as pastors, ministers, deacons, trustees, teachers, and missionaries. The grandchild whom my grandfather loved the most is thankful, grateful, and appreciative for all his grandfather did for him and the entire family.

Bibliography

Allen, Jr., O. Wesley, *Preaching in the Era of Trump,*
Nashville, TN: Chalice Press, 2017.

Allen, Ronald J., *Thinking Theologically: The Preacher as Theologian,*
Minneapolis, MN: Fortress Press, 2007.

Anderson, Herbert and Foley, Edward, *Mighty Stories, Dangerous Rituals: Weaving Together*
the Human and the Divine, San Francisco, CA: Jossey-Bass, A Wiley Company, 1998.

Bailey, Randall C., *They Were All Together in One Place: Toward Minority Biblical Criticism,*
Atlanta, GA: Society of Biblical Literature, 2009.

Bogart, Anne, *And Then, You Act: Making Art in an Unpredictable World,*
Oxfordshire, UK: Routledge Press, 2007.

Booth, Wayne C., *Craft of Research, Fourth Edition, The*,
Chicago, IL: The University of Chicago Press, 2016.

Brooks, Gennifer Benjamin, *Good News Preaching: Offering the Gospel in Every Sermon,*
Cleveland, OH: Pilgrim Press, 2009.

Brown, Teresa L. Frye, *Delivering the Sermon: Voice, Body, and Animation in Proclamation,*
Minneapolis, MN: Fortress Press, 2008.

Brown, Teresa L. Frye, *Weary Throats and New Songs: Black Women Proclaiming God's Word,*
Nashville, TN: Abingdon Press, 2003.

Brueggemann, Walter, *The Practice of Prophetic Imagination: Preaching an Emancipating Word,* Minneapolis, MN: Fortress Press, 2012.

Chilcote, Paul W. and Laceye C. Warner, editors, *The Study of Evangelism: Exploring a Missional Practice of the Church*, Grand Rapids, MI: William B. Eerdmans Publishing Company, 2008.

Copeland, K. Edward, *Riding in the Second Chariot: A Guide for Associate Ministers*, Kankakee, IL: PrayerCloset Publishing, 1999.

Cosgrove, Charles H., and W. Dow Edgerton, foreword by Don M. Wardlaw, *In Other Words: Incarnational Translation for Preaching*, Grand Rapids, MI: William B. Eerdmans Publishing Company, 2007.
Cox, Meg E., editor, *Cynicism and Hope: Reclaiming Discipleship in a Postdemocratic Society*, Eugene, OR: Cascade Books, 2009.

Creswell, John W., and Johanna Creswell, *30 Essential Skills for the Qualitative Researcher, Second Edition*, Thousand Oaks, CA: Sage Publishing, 2021.

Creswell, John W., and Cheryl N. Poth, *Qualitative Inquiry & Research Design, Fourth Edition*, Thousand Oaks, CA: Sage Publishing, 2018.

Drummond, Sarah, *Holy Clarity: The Practice of Planning and Evaluation,* New York, NY: Rowman and Littlefield Publishers, 2009.

Ellison II, Greggory, *Fearless Dialogues: A New Movement for Justice,* Nashville, TN: Westminster John Knox Press, 2017.

Evans, Tony, *Kingdom Disciples: Heaven's Representatives on Earth,*

Nashville, TN: LifeWay Press, 2008.

Gilbert, Kenyatta R., *Exodus Preaching: Crafting Sermons about Justice and Hope*,
Nashville, TN: Abingdon Press, 2018.

Harris, James H., *Word Made Plain, The: the Power and Promise of Preaching*,
Minneapolis, MN: Fortress Press, 2004.

Helsel, Carolyn B., *Preaching about Racism: A Guide for Faith Leaders*,
St. Louis, MO: Chalice Press, 2018.

Hicks, Donna, "Introduction: A New Model of Dignity," *Dignity: The Essential Role It Plays in*
Resolving Conflict, New Haven, CT: Yale University Press, 2011.

Hicks, Donna, "The 10 Essential Elements of Dignity," *Dignity: The Essential Role It Plays in*
Resolving Conflict, New Haven, CT: Yale University Press, 2011.

Honeycutt, Frank, *Preaching for Adult Conversion and Commitment: Invitation to a Life*
Transformed, Nashville, TN: Abingdon Press, 2000.

Jay-Z, *Decoded*,
New York, NY: Spiegel & Grau, 2nd Edition, November 2011.

Jones, Kirk Byron, *Jazz of Preaching: How to Preach with Great Freedom and Joy, The*,
Nashville, TN: Abingdon Press, 2004.

King, Jr., Martin Luther, "Beyond Vietnam: A Time to Break Silence,"
Riverside Church, New York City, April 4, 1967),
https://www.crmvet.org/info/mlk_viet.pdf, assessed on June 8, 2023.

Lamott, Anne, *Bird by Bird: Some Instructions on Writing and Life*, New York, NY: Anchor Books, 1995.

LaRue, Cleophus J., *Heart of Black Preaching, The*,
    Louisville, KY: Westminster John Knox Press, 2000.

LaRue, Cleophus J., *Re-Thinking Celebration: From Rhetoric to Praise in African American*
Preaching, Louisville, KY: Westminster John Knox Press, 2016.

Lord, Jennifer L., *Finding Language and Imagery: Elements of Preaching* series. O. Wesley
Allen Jr., series editor, Minneapolis, MN: Fortress Press, 2010.

Lozado, Francisco, *Soundings in Cultural Criticism: Perspectives and Methods in Culture,*
Power, and Identity in the New Testament, Minneapolis, MN: Augsburg Press, 2013.

Markusse, Gabi, foreword by Paul Middleton, *Salvation in the Gospel of Mark: The Death of*
Jesus and the Path of Discipleship, Eugene, OR: Pickwick Publications, 2018.

McClure, John S., *Ethical Approaches to Preaching: Choose the Best Way to Preach about*
Difficult Issues, Nashville, TN: Cascade Books, 2021.

McKesson, DeRay, "Bully and the Pulpit," *On the Other Side of Freedom: The Case of Hope*,
New York, NY: Viking Press, 2018.

McLean, Bradley H., *Biblical Interpretation and Philosophical Hermeneutics*,
Cambridge: Cambridge University Press, 2012.

McMickle, Marvin, *Where Have All the Prophets Gone: Reclaiming Prophetic Preaching in*
America, Holbrook, NY: Pilgrim Press, 2019.

McMickle, Marvin A., ed. André Resner, Jr., "Preaching in the Face of Economic Injustice," *Just Preaching: Prophetic Voices for Economic Justice*, St. Louis, MO: Chalice Press, 2003.

Moss III, Otis, *Preach!: The Power and Purpose Behind Our Praise,* Holbrook, NY: Pilgrim Press, 2012.

Newson, Ryan Andrew, *Cut in Stone: Confederate Monuments and Theological Disruption,* Waco, TX: Baylor University Press, 2020.

Powell, Mark Allen, *What Do They Hear: Building Bridges Between Pulpit and Pew,* Nashville, TN: Abingdon Press, 2007.

Proctor, Samuel D., foreword by Gardner C. Taylor, *The Certain Sound of the Trumpet: Crafting a Sermon of Authority*, Valley Forge, PA: Judson Press, 1994.

Rediger, G. Lloyd, *Clergy Killers: Guidance for Pastors and Congregations Under Attack,* Inver Grove Heights, MN: Logos Productions, Inc., 1997.

Resner, Jr., André, ed. André Resner, Jr., "Preaching's Purpose: Thoughts on Message and Method," *Just Preaching: Prophetic Voices for Economic Justice*, St. Louis: Chalice Press, 2003.

Sande, Ken, *The Peacemaker: A Biblical Guide to Resolving Personal Conflict, Third Edition,* Grand Rapids, MI: Baker Books, 2004.

Schade, Leah D., *Preaching in the Purple Zone: Preaching Across the Red-Blue Divide,* Lanham, MD: Rowman and Littlefield Publishers, 2019.

Schnase, Robert, *"Five Practices of a Fruitful Congregation,"* Nashville, TN: Abingdon Press, 2018.

Sensing, Tim, *Qualitative Research: A Multi-Methods Approach to Projects for Doctor of*
Ministry Theses, Eugene, OR: Wipf & Stock Publishers, Illustrated Edition, 2011.

Thomas, Frank A., forward by Will Willimon, *God of the Dangerous Sermon, The,*
Nashville, TN: Abingdon Press, 2021.

Thomas, Frank A., *How to Preach Dangerous Sermon,*
Nashville, TN: Abingdon Press, 2021.

Thomas, Frank A., *Introduction to the Practice of African American Preaching,*
Nashville, TN: Abingdon Press, 2016.

Thomas, Frank A. *Preaching as Celebration Digital Lecture Series and Workbook,*
Indianapolis, IN: Hope for Life International, Inc., 2014.

Thomas, Frank A., *They Like to Never Quit Praisin' God: The Role of Celebration in Preaching,*
Cleveland, OH: Pilgrim Press, 2013.

Thompson, Lisa L., *Ingenuity: Preaching as an Outsider,*
Nashville, TN: Abingdon Press, 2018.

Thompson, Lisa, *Preaching the Headlines: Possibilities and Pitfalls,*
Minneapolis, MN: Fortress Press, 2021.

Tisdale, Nora Tubbs, *Prophetic Preaching: A Pastoral Approach,*
Louisville, KY: Westminster John Knox Press, 2021.

Turabian, Kate, *A Manual for Writers of Research Papers, theses, and Dissertations, Eighth*

Edition: Chicago Style for Students and Researchers, Chicago, IL: University of Chicago Press, 2013.

Vine, Cedric E.W., *Jesus and the Nations: Discipleship and Mission in the Gospel of Matthew*,
    Eugene, OR: Pickwick Publications, 2022.

Vyhmeister, Nancy Jean, *Quality Research Papers,*
Grand Rapids, MI: Zondervan Press, 2008.

Williams, Rowan, *Being Christian: Bible, Baptism, Eucharist, Prayer,*
    Grand Rapids, MI: Eerdmans Publishing, 2014.
Wiseman, Karyn L. *I Refuse to Preach a Boring Sermon! Engaging the 21st Century Listener*,
Cleveland, OH: Pilgrim Press. 2013.

Appendices

Appendix A

United States[105] Total Population (fig #1)

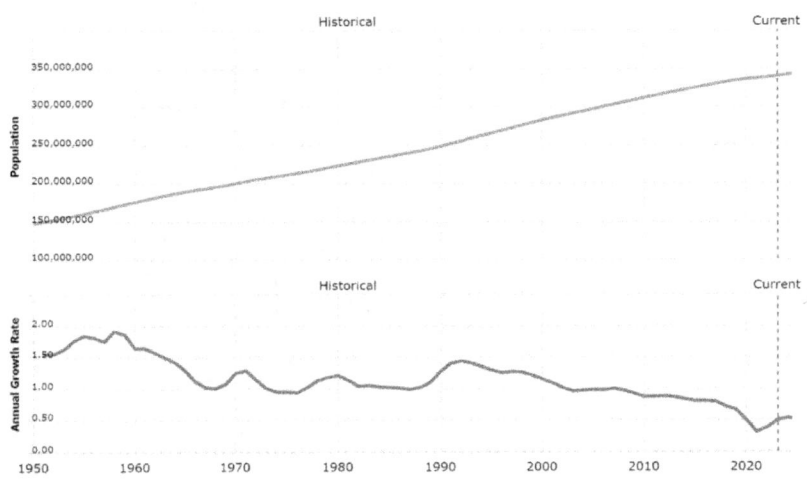

[105] "United States of America," Data Source: United Nations-World Population Prospects, U.S. Population 1950-2023, https://macrotrends.net/countries/USA/united-states/population, assessed on October 27, 2023.

St. Paul,[106] MN Total Population (Fig#5)

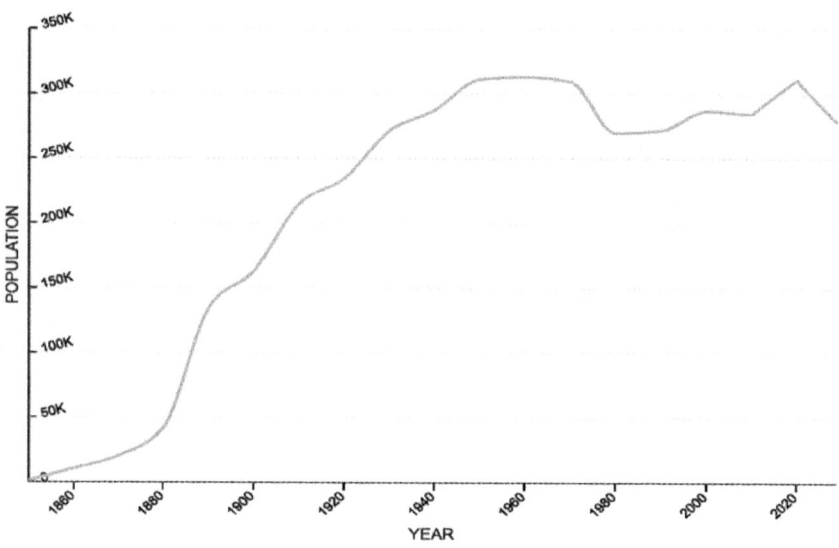

[106] "St. Paul, MN," https://worldpopulationreview.com/us-cities/st-paul-mn-population, assessed on October 27, 2023.

Appendix B

1. What was the title and scripture text of the sermon?

2. Was the sermon easy to follow?

3. Was the theme of the sermon clear? If so, what was it?

4. On a scale of 0 - 5, did the title of the sermon accurately reflect the content of the sermon? (5 = highest)

5. On a scale of 0 - 5, was the content of the sermon anchored in the sermonic text?
   (5 = highest)

6. On a scale of 0 - 5, how clear was the objective of the sermon? (5 = highest)

7. What did you learn from the sermon and how has it impacted your life?

8. What would you recommend to the preacher to make the sermon content better?

9. What would you recommend to the preacher to make the sermon delivery better?

10. Was the audience the right audience for this message?

Appendix C

Ministry Engagement Survey/Questionnaire

All survey responses will remain anonymous and will not be tracked back to any individual.

The survey responses will be used and evaluated to be included in an academic thesis for publication.

1. **On a scale of 1-7, how important to you is your involvement in church ministry? (Choose One)**

   1 2 3 4 5 6 7

2. **Do you leave services feeling spiritually fed? (Choose one)**

   Yes. The services fill me spiritually.

   Often. I know the pastor/church has my best interest at heart.

   Sometimes. I feel the services aren't as relevant to me as they could be.

   Rarely. I'm feeling disconnected from the services for personal reasons.

   I'm feeling disconnected because of the doctrine being taught.

3. **Do you feel Pilgrim Baptist Church is sensitive to the major needs of congregants? (Choose one)**

   Yes. I've seen the church help people with real needs.

   Yes. I've been the recipient of help from the church when I needed it.

   Yes. I've heard the pastor/church express a desire to help congregants.

I'm unsure.

No. I've experienced a major need, or seen others with needs, and felt that nobody noticed.

4. **Do you feel Pilgrim Baptist Church spends money in a way that aligns with its mission? (Choose one)**

Yes. I feel they're spending money on things that really matter.

I feel they could be more careful in their spending.

I don't know where they're spending and would like to understand it so I can feel engaged in the initiatives.

I don't believe church spending is something I need to be concerned with.

5. **Do you know or have an idea of what your spiritual gift(s) is/are?**

Yes.

No.

If yes, what is/are your spiritual gift(s)?

_____

_____

_____

6. **Do you feel engaged in Pilgrim Baptist Church? (Choose one)**

Yes. I feel very engaged in the church, its mission, and initiatives.

Yes. I feel engaged in the church.

I enjoy being in the church, but don't take an active role.

Sometimes I feel like I'm watching from the sidelines.

I don't feel engaged.

7. **Do you feel welcomed at Pilgrim Baptist Church? (Choose one)**

Yes. The pastor makes me feel welcomed.

Yes. The other congregants make me feel welcomed.

Yes. Both the pastor and other congregants make me feel welcomed.

I don't feel welcome.

8. **We're planning to implement several small groups, programs, or events in the next six months, and want to get a count of possible participants. Which of the following would you most likely attend? (Choose as many as you like)**

A mom's group.

A father's group.

Marriage and relationship classes.

A youth mission trip focused on building faith for the future.

A scripture exploration group.

An evangelism group

A spiritual gift discernment group

Other _____

Not interested in attending at this time

9. **We can help individuals in the local shelter this winter but need more resources to make the biggest impact on**

their lives. Which way would you be most able to contribute? (Choose as many as you like)

Taking a turn in the soup kitchen.

Donating clothing.

Donating food.

Making cash donations.

Any of the above.

Circumstances prevent me from contributing at this time.

Not interested in contributing at this time

10. **If you started attending Pilgrim Baptist Church in the last year, what's mainly responsible for bringing you through the doors for the first time? (Choose as many as you like)**

A friend or family member.

Posts or ads on social media.

A special event or program.

I saw the building and was curious.

An online search.

Pilgrim's website

I've been attending for longer than a year.

11. **What church ministry group are you most interested in participating in? (Choose as many as you like)**

Women's Ministry

Men's Ministry

Music Ministry

Fine Arts' Ministry

Ushers' Ministry

Finance Ministry

Christian Education Ministry

Youth Ministry

Evangelism Ministry

Deacon's Ministry

Associate Minister's Ministry

Other: _____

Other: _____

Other: _____

I am not interested in participating at this time

12. **On a scale of 1-7, how important to you is it that the church offers virtual ministries and memberships? (Choose one)**

   1 2 3 4 5 6 7

13. **What is your annual income? (Choose one)**

   Less than $20,000

   $20,001 - $50,000

   $50,001 - $80,000

   $80,001 - $125,000

   $125,001 - $200,000

   More than $200,000

   Prefer not to say.

14. **What is your employment status? (Choose one)**

   Full-time

   Part-time

Currently seeking opportunities

Retired

Prefer not to say.

15. How many dependents do you have? (Choose one)

0-2

3-5

6 or more

Prefer not to say.

16. What is your age? (Choose one)

Under 25

26 - 35

36 - 45

46 - 55

56 - 75

Over 76

Prefer not to say.

17. Are you a member of Pilgrim Baptist Church? (Choose one)

Yes

No

Prefer not to say.

18. Are you a member of any church or organized religious organization? (Choose one)

1.   Yes

2.   No

3.   Prefer not to say

4.   If   yes,   which   church/organization?

_____

19. What is your marital status? (Choose one)

Married

Single

Divorced

Widowed

Separated

Prefer not to say.

20. What is your highest educational pursuit? (Choose one)

High school diploma/GED

Trade school certificate

Associate's degree

Bachelor's degree

Master's degree

Doctorate/PhD degree.

Prefer not to say.

21. What is your gender? (Choose one)

Male

Female

Prefer not to say.

About the Author

I was born in Aberdeen, Mississippi on July 21, 1968. I was baptized by total immersion at the age of seven at the Zion Spring Missionary Baptist Church, Egypt, MS, by Rev. Dr. Michael Lee Perry. From an early age I have always been actively engaged in the ministry of every church I was blessed to be a member. While at the Zion Spring M.B. Church in Egypt, MS, I served as an usher, sang in the choir, frequently attended Bible Study, Sunday school classes, Vacation Bible School, and Baptist Training Union. My grandparents and mother also served as great resources and modeled for me what engaging in the ministry of the church looked like. Both of my grandfathers served as deacons at Zion Spring, sang in the choir, and were frequents attendees in Sunday School and Bible Study. Both of my grandmothers served in the served in the missionary society, sang in the choir, taught Sunday School, and attended Bible Study frequently.

In July 1990 I was hired as an electrical engineer by the Minnesota Mining and Manufacturing Company in St. Paul, MN after graduating from Northwestern University, Evanston, IL with a Bachelor of Science degree in Electrical Engineering. I joined the Pilgrim Baptist Church in St. Paul, MN in September 1993. I served as the audio/video technical director and website designer. I served on the Trustee Board and taught Sunday School and Bible study. Upon returning to Pilgrim Baptist Church in 2019, I currently teach

Bible Study, taught a course on discipleship, and serve as an associate minister to the senior pastor. In that role I have assisted and completed various tasks as directed by the pastor. I am currently working with the pastor on a- plan to increase church membership by inviting the community at large to join the church. As part of the plan, I will be creating a team of church members to go door to door to every house in a one square mile area around the church to invite them to church, interview them to find out what some of their daily needs are, identify how Pilgrim can address those needs, and to discover what hindrances are preventing them from joining Pilgrim Baptist Church.

I first sensed a call to preach the gospel of Jesus Christ my senior year of high school. I ignored the vision initially, but it was always present within my spirit. In February 1995 I had another vision I could not ignore. For over two years I struggled with the idea of preaching the gospel because I did not want to be a preacher. I was content with my life at the time and did not want to make a life-changing decision to disrupt my current life trajectory. On December 7, 1997, I accepted my call into the gospel ministry. I preached my first public sermon on May 10, 1998, titled "Jesus Christ Is Lord" taken from Matthew 28:16-20; Mark 16:19-20 at Pilgrim Baptist Church, St. Paul, MN. Despite my initial reluctance and apprehension, I am blessed and highly favored to celebrate twenty-five years of preaching the gospel of Jesus Christ. When I accepted my call to preach the gospel of Jesus Christ, I never wanted to be the best preacher of all time. However, I did want to be the best preacher I could possibly be. I am attempting to do everything within my power to achieve that goal. In addition to praying, reading scripture, relying on the Holy Spirit for inspiration, meditating, believing in my call, I am continually expanding my personal theology with as much diversity as possible. I completed the Master of Divinity degree at a Lutheran seminary and the Doctor of Ministry degree at a Methodist seminary. When I see my Lord and Savior, Jesus Christ, face to face, I want to be able to truthfully say that I preached his Word to the best of my ability. I try to approach every sermon I preach as if it was the last sermon I would ever preach. Preaching and teaching the Word of God are two of greatest joys in my life. Whenever I preach and teach, I normally stay on spiritual high for about an hour after the preaching or teaching session has ended. Preaching and teaching are at least two spiritual gifts that I currently have been gifted by the Holy Spirit.

In November 2001 I began serving as the senior pastor of the New Bethel Baptist Church in Manly, IA. In addition to preaching and teaching on a weekly basis, some of my pastoral accomplishment highlights were implementing a new electronic financial records system, streamlining the membership records system, conducting Vacation Bible School sessions, and completed the requirements for New Bethel to renew their membership to the Iowa Missionary and Educational Baptist State Convention. I resigned as senior pastor in June 2017 and returned to Pilgrim Baptist Church in St. Paul, MN as an associate minister.

The four churches I am currently most connected to and

associated with are Zion Springs Missionary Baptist Church, Okolona, MS, New Hebron Missionary Baptist Church, Aberdeen, MS, Pilgrim Baptist Church, St. Paul, MN, and New Bethel Baptist Church, Manly, IA. I preached the three first year sermons at Zion Springs and New Hebron. Both churches were instrumental in my early childhood development. Both churches supported me emotionally and financially when I graduated high school, attended, and graduated from college. Both churches contributed and participated in my development from my youth growing up in the church, to supporting me through my undergraduate college pursuits, and throughout my spiritual growth and ministry as a preacher and pastor.